MIRACLES IN BULGARIA

ALLAN HORSFIELD

WITH INSIGHTS INTO WHEN AND HOW TO PRAY FOR HEALING.

Trafford PUBLISHING

Order this book online at www.trafford.com/07-1054
or email orders@trafford.com

Most Trafford titles are also available at major online book retailers.

Note for Librarians: A cataloguing record for this book is available from Library and Archives Canada at www.collectionscanada.ca/amicus/index-e.html

Printed in Victoria, BC, Canada.

ISBN: 978-1-4251-2961-3

Cover Photograph by Richard Ammon

We at Trafford believe that it is the responsibility of us all, as both individuals and corporations, to make choices that are environmentally and socially sound. You, in turn, are supporting this responsible conduct each time you purchase a Trafford book, or make use of our publishing services. To find out how you are helping, please visit www.trafford.com/responsiblepublishing.html

Our mission is to efficiently provide the world's finest, most comprehensive book publishing service, enabling every author to experience success. To find out how to publish your book, your way, and have it available worldwide, visit us online at www.trafford.com/10510

Trafford PUBLISHING

www.trafford.com

North America & international
toll-free: 1 888 232 4444 (USA & Canada)
phone: 250 383 6864 • fax: 250 383 6804
email: info@trafford.com

The United Kingdom & Europe
phone: +44 (0)1865 722 113 • local rate: 0845 230 9601
facsimile: +44 (0)1865 722 868 • email: info.uk@trafford.com

10 9 8 7 6 5 4 3 2

PREFACE

This little book is a very personal account of some of the people I met and the things God did in Bulgaria. I visited the town of Troyan in the Central Highlands between 2 and 4 times each year from 1998 to 2002.

I never had any intention of writing a book. I made no notes or diary. As a result, many of the things that happened and people I met have since been forgotten. In fact almost everything would have been lost in my memory, except for the Lord's intervention. In December 2006 during a period of 5 sleepless nights, forgotten memories of people and prayer and healings and conversations came rolling through my mind. At the end of those 5 nights I knew I had to make a record of what the Lord had reminded me.

I would like to thank Annette, my wife, for the practical help and support she gave me, and her willingness to allow me to keep 'disappearing' to Troyan. Also to my long-standing friend and prayer partner, Dr. Andrew Williamson, who willingly accompanied me annually to Troyan, and gave such wise advice and insight. My thanks to Christo and Margarita Petkov for their hospitality and friendship, and to Pastor Peter Peevsky under whose authority and support much healing was done. Above all, my thanks are due to Vasil and Katia Marinova. They were willing to give up their time completely when I visited. Vasil held home and family together and generously and unselfishly released his wife to be part of this ministry. Katya was both my translator and co-counsellor. This book does not do justice to her personal contribution, especially when praying with the women. Without her total commitment none of this could have taken place.

The following is my record of those memories given back to me by the Lord. It is also a journey through the many lessons I learnt about healing. It is my hope and prayer that these memories will be as much an instruction and insight to others as they have been to me.

Allan Horsfield

April 2007

Contents

PREFACE 3

INTRODUCTION 9

1. HITTING THE GROUND RUNNING 13
   Kalinka 17
   The Thursday Evening Meeting 24

2. BULGARIAN HOSPITALITY 27
   Bojana 29
   Kalinka's Parents 30
   Donka 31

3 MY FIRST SUNDAY 35
   Peshka 39

4. MY SECOND VISIT. 43
   Four Miracles 45
   An Elderly Saint 48
   Vilena And Ville 49

5. THE GYPSIES 51
   Milena 52
   A Gypsy Feast 54
   Jifca 57
   Enka's Squint 60
   A Problem Of Anger 64

6. FOUR INSTITUTIONS OF TROYAN 69
   The Orphanage 69
   The High School 70
   The Hospital 70
   The Prison 73

7. THE RESTAURANT 77
   The New Pastor 78
   Donka's Departing 79
   The Gypsy Church 80

8.	DESPERATION	83
	The Woman WithVvitaligo	83
	A Crippled Baby	86
	A Dying Man	87
	Bobby	92
9.	A SECOND PENTECOSTAL CHURCH	95
	Christo And Maggie's Hospitality	99
	From Needs To Wants	100
10.	THE IMPORTANCE OF REPENTANCE	103
	A Man Into Witchcraft.	103
	The Teenager With A Strapped Back	104
	The Elderly Lady With A Throat Problem	105
	Maya	106
11.	MY LAST VISIT TO TROYAN	111
	My Final Sermon	112

This book is dedicated to
Vasil and Katya Marinova

INTRODUCTION

My story begins with another book. In 1996 I took one year off work to research my first book – "The Four Horseman of John's Apocalypse". This work had nothing to do with healing or counselling. It was an in depth overview of the History of the Twentieth Century from God's viewpoint. It sought to expose the devastating effects of the release into history of four demonic principalities – Communism, Fascism, Materialism and Islam. The effects of their scourge on mankind is described in Revelation 6:1-8.

During my painstaking research into this I noted and made mention of hundreds of places around the world. One tiny note was made of Troyan in Bulgaria: "the building now used as a Sunday School had been a place of torture and interrogation of believers by the Communists". The word "Troyan" stuck in my mind. Even after the book was written, and I was freed from 'wrestling' with its contents, "Troyan" would not leave my mind.

I prayed about this and wondered if God was calling me to go to this place. The more I prayed the more I felt the Lord was saying to me: "go to the Church in Troyan and pray for them; also go to the Hospital." I didn't know what to do with this, but help soon came. During a November Sunday morning meeting, my Pastor invited people to come to the front and share any blessings or prayer needs they had. I sank back in my chair! "I'll let the others go," I thought to myself. Unfortunately no one moved. On the rare occasions when this happened the Pastor would always move on. On this occasion he didn't. Instead he persisted and made the request again. "Someone, I believe, has something to share" he confidently announced. Reluctantly I walked to the front.

"I don't know whether this is from the Lord or whether I'm going through a midlife crisis," I began. "For the last 12 months the name of "Troyan" has not left my mind, and recently I've felt God speaking to me about going to the Church in Troyan. Please would you pray about this and share with me your honest feelings. I am very willing to be shown to be making a mistake!"

With much embarrassment I sat down. Immediately two Church members came to the front and responded positively. One shared relevant Scriptures that had been on her heart the previous week. After the meeting three others came and each gave positive encouragement. One had a burden for Bulgaria and had been praying for that country for six months! Everyone was saying "go!"

I turned to my wife while driving home: "Five people can't all be wrong. It's as strong a confirmation as I could ever ask for. I have to go."

Within days I had booked a return flight to Sophia, Bulgaria's Capital City. This was for the following February when I had free time from my Craft Jewellery business. Finally I looked on the map to find out where exactly Troyan was. To my surprise it was a small town in the mountains, in the middle of nowhere!

I flew out on a cold Tuesday morning. I planned to stay the first night in the Capital, giving me the time to find the bus for Troyan. I found the name of a Sofia hotel from a travel guide, but finding a bus to Troyan was a little more difficult. Hardly anyone in Sofia seemed to speak a word of English – especially the taxi drivers! And there were a number of bus stations, scattered in different parts of the city. Everyone I spoke to seemed as confused as myself! It took half a day to sort it all out.

Finally, at Noon on the Wednesday, with my large suitcase safely packed in the hold, I boarded the bus. I reconfirmed with three of my fellow passengers: "Troyan?" "Da"…… "Da"……

The old bus exploded into action, coughing and rattling onto the highway, and narrowly avoiding a large pothole the size of a small car. It was a lovely spring like day, with warm sunshine. The winter valleys and hills looked so beautiful. The mountains were high and noble and unspoilt. I could have been in the Alps, but for the sight of the small village communities. They showed off the real poverty of the land; old men driving their donkey carts, children attending to the family cow or pig, wooden houses with shoddily repaired straw roofs, mud homes built in the 'wattle and daub' manner still housing families, shepherds leading a handful of sheep up dirt roads to meagre patches of grass, gardens utilised in every way to contribute to family mealtimes, unreplaced tiles blown off roofs, broken windows and doors. Pavements and other structures seemed in complete disarray, abandoned from their now forgotten original intended purpose. Behind these humble dwellings I was about to discover that every home was an extended household, housing at least three generations. I was travelling back in time to a standard of living last seen in England before the Great War.

It was bewildering to be so suddenly propelled into this foreign land, and a rural culture and trappings from a medieval age. What was I doing here? I didn't know. I was simply holding on to God's word for me, confirmed by five Church members. What was God doing?

Chapter One

HITTING THE GROUND RUNNING

I stumbled off the old bus onto the derelict piece of gravel-covered land that was the Troyan Bus Station. It was now teatime. I had been travelling to an unknown destination in an unknown land and I was tired.

The next challenge was to find a Hotel. I could leave the search for the Pastor's house until the morning. I noticed parked on the side of the road nearby a couple of battered cars that advertised a "taxi" service. The first one in particular caught my eye – a distressed 25 years old golden Mercedes! I approached the driver with a smile. Body language is very important when you are a stranger in a foreign land. Showing friendship prior to speaking breaks down barriers.

"Hotel?" I asked.

"Hotel?" he answered, looking both bemused and confused.

"Yes"

His hand came up to wave me on, rejecting the fare; but I persisted.

We set off, and after about 150 metres stopped. We had arrived at the only Hotel in Troyan. His hand gestures had not been a refusal of the fare, but rather an attempt at giving me directions! He was encouraging me to save the money and walk the 150 metres. In contrast to the mercenary tactics of the Sofia taxi drivers, here was a kindly old man looking after me. He refused my money for the short ride, but I insisted. For the next year, until I began to hire and drive my own car from Sofia Airport, he became my personal 'chauffeur'. He took me everywhere, and always patiently waited for the return journey. The Lord was already providing for my needs. .

I entered the Hotel. What a contrast with Sofia! It appeared unloved, unkempt, unclean, and unused. Obviously a remnant from the Communist times, this had once been a quality place to stay. It had entertained high-ranking Army officers and Government officials and even Soviet visitors who came to the Bulgarian mountains to hunt. Now the Hotel had no longer any purpose or paying customers – it had lost the will to live! The handful of visitors who came to Troyan stayed with family or friends. No one in the mountains had money for a Hotel; and foreign tourists never noticed the signpost to Troyan. They kept on the road to the Western-standard Holiday Resorts of the Black Sea.

After shouting "hello" a few times I finally gained some reluctant attention. I handed over some money for 2 nights and was shown to my room. The hotel had long since been stripped of anything sellable, so I was grateful to find one set of sheets and blankets and a small towel. The soap I brought with me, in anticipation of 'shortages'!

It was getting dark and cold. The empty hotel was silent and eerie. I heard no one. I was the only guest, and the isolation was depressing. Was this a foolish mistake I had embarked upon? How embarrassing it would be to return home and admit to a mistake. And even if I did meet with the Pastor, how would we speak? Nobody understood a word of English! Yet every time such doubts came to me, I was reminded of the five testimonies of my Church friends. I could be, and often was, wrong. Stepping out in faith requires us to risk being wrong! – but not all those five as well. No, I reassured myself, this was where the Lord wanted me to be, for reasons I didn't know. Tomorrow I would begin to find out.

I went for a walk in the cool dark evening air. I have visited many countries, in Europe and Asia. One thing I love to do in a strange town or city is walk around it – everywhere. Especially I love the tropical climate of South East Asia. The cooler evenings are the time when everything happens. The streets are noisy and alive with shoppers, people eating, children playing, old people chatting. But Troyan was different. Although the town was enjoying one of the warmest February evenings on record, the place was dark, silent and uninviting. The inadequate street lamps shone onto silent and empty streets. Was there still a curfew in this place after dark? There was neither people nor traffic. Few had cars and even fewer could afford to use them. I had nothing and no one to smile at. In Asia people love foreigners, especially Westerners. Children show off their shy smiles and giggle. Young people want to practise speaking English. Cheeky little boys shout out: "Hello. How are you?" But on this first evening in Troyan I was invisible.

A chorus of cocks crowing awakened me. It was a crisp sunny morning. The night had passed in silence apart from an occasional shout from somewhere in the 'catacombs' below. I felt like a monk in his cell, with only the Lord for conversation.

"Now what do I do?" I thought, half talking to myself and half asking the Lord. As I was clueless, I directed my thoughts and questions to Him: " Lord, I don't mind being a fool for you, but please fulfil your Word today. Open a door for me to meet the Pastor."

I had travelled from England with a name and an address. But it seemed of little use when no one appeared to speak a word of English. Then I remembered walking past a Pharmacy the evening before. Perhaps they could help. I went to see. At last a breakthrough! The lady Pharmacist immediately understood my plight, wrote down the address in Bulgarian, and gestured for me to get a taxi. .

I walked off, somehow knowing my taxi man would be waiting for me at the Bus Station – and he was! Was this God's provision of an angel in a golden chariot at my service? An angel he may not have been, but God's provision it certainly was. I gave him the tiny scrap of paper and he eyes shone in recognition. He smiled a smile that seemed to say that now he understood what I was doing in Troyan.

The old Merc trundled along the High Street, and then turned a sharp right up a small but steep hillside. The road changed from smooth tarmac to undulating and badly laid concrete. Ancient concrete. The surface had been repaired and repaired again. A combination of soviet-style misappropriation (in this case of cement!), together with the lack of adequate drainage, had destroyed the surface, leaving deep gutters and potholes. But my old chauffeur was a master at avoiding axle damage and within minutes we were outside Number 34A Prespa Street.

I stood outside the Pastor's little house. It was 10.00a.m. I was an unknown, unannounced and unexpected guest. I rang the bell. The door opened and an elderly lady appeared and approached me, followed by her daughter holding her little boy.

However stupid it would sound, I had to introduce myself immediately.

"Hello," I started, "I'm sorry to bother you. My name is Allan. I've come from England to visit you."

It was obvious from her facial expression that the older lady could not understand a word. Confused, she turned to her daughter...

"Oh, please come in..." was the young woman's immediate response.

I climbed six high steps to the front door, abandoned my shoes, and went in. The small room immediately reminded me of my childhood home in West Yorkshire. There my parents, two sisters and I lived in a tiny house with two bedrooms and one room downstairs – plus the cellar. Just as with my boyhood in the 1950's this small room was a kitchen, dining room, sitting room, and occasionally bedroom. A large square dining table staked its claim in the middle..

The three of us sat down. There was Nanka, Pastor Peter's wife; Katya, her English-speaking daughter; and two year old Ivan, her son. I wasted no time in telling my story: how God had spoken to me to come to the Church in Troyan; how this was confirmed by my congregation; how an address had miraculously been provided; and how I had found the place. As the tale unfolded tears filled their eyes.

When I had finished, Katya told me how her Church had been praying for four years for contact and partnership with a Western Church. They had introduced themselves to a Swiss Church, but found themselves unwanted simply because they were Bulgarians. And now from nowhere I had suddenly appeared! I seemed an answer to their prayers.

We talked for about half an hour, Katya stopping regularly to translate to her mother. In this small house with one sitting room and three bedrooms lived Pastor Peter and his wife Nanka; Katya, her husband Vasil and son Ivan; Katya's sister, Valentina, with her husband Krasimir and four year old son Angel; and Katya's brother, Emanuel. Three families in one tiny house.

Katya's father was out but would be home later. Although the leader of the Church, he was in fact a senior elder acting as Pastor. The Church was small and poor and it was difficult to find a fully trained Pastor. The Communist Government, while tolerating older Pastors, had not allowed younger men to train. As a result the production of new men to replace the elderly had dried up. New Pastors were now being trained, but they were outnumbered by the vacancies. They had the pick of the crop, and usually chose the bigger and livelier Churches in the cities and larger towns. Troyan was being passed by.

After a hurried 30 minutes of conversation, we were out of time. Katya had arranged to go and visit her friend Kalinka who was in Hospital. I quickly asked if I could come too. I had half a suitcase of medicines to give to the Hospital, and it seemed the perfect opportunity to make an appointment to see the Hospital Director. We walked the ten-minute walk back to the Bus Station, where my taxi was waiting. The lift was much appreciated, as the Hospital was a forty-minute walk away.

At last the taxi driver could satisfy his curiosity. He asked Katya more and more questions, which she openly answered. In Troyan, better give a little information than none at all! Having understood my business, he seemed all the more eager to help. He parked us near the entrance and happily waited to return us home.

February in Bulgaria is notoriously cold. Troyan lies deep in the Central Mountains where temperatures can plummet to minus 20 degrees C. Of course, I had been totally ignorant of such potential extremes when booking my flights. There should have been a thick layer of snow covering Troyan, making it extremely difficult to move around. I should have been freezing with inadequate clothes and shoes (I only ever travelled to Troyan in open-toed sandals!). But God had provided for me. 1998 had the warmest February on record; and I had come during the warmest week! So warm was it that patients and staff at the Hospital were walking and relaxing in the grounds of the building, enjoying the spring sunshine.

KALINKA

Kalinka was happy to see us but looked weak and exhausted. We walked a little in the grounds as Katya introduced me and shared my story. We sat down on the grass in our own private place. How wonderful God is. In the Hospital it would have been impossible to talk privately.

From my very first question I realised how utterly dependent I was on Katya, not only for translation, but also for partnership. Another translator might have translated the words, but conveyed doubt or questions about my approach. Katya never did. She was utterly faithful to both the words and the spirit of what was being done. She understood the Biblical principles behind what I did, and regularly explained them when confusion arose. We were both about to learn new things, and would each be blessed by it. The partnership worked from the first question, and continued for four and a half years.

Katya was a blessing for me in other ways. As a life-long member of the Church she knew almost everyone who came to me in my first two years, and still knew many more after that. By her own example, and as the Pastor's daughter, she was respected and trusted in a way few others were. As many of those we prayed with would be women, she was able to put her arms around them and comfort them and speak to them in ways I could not. Above all, they trusted Katya's compassion and discretion.

Kalinka was a young 26 years old woman who had spent the previous five years of her young life in and out of the Troyan Hospital. She suffered from stomach ulcers – a rare occurrence in a young woman. The severity would ease at times, but always return. When we visited, her latest attack was very serious; even with the Hospital medication Kalinka had been unable to eat for three days.

The Church and Christian friends had all prayed for five years, but no amount of prayer had helped. I wanted to know more, so asked her to tell me her story,

Kalinka had married when she was only nineteen years old. She went to live with her husband's family who were not Christians. Her mother-in-law had taken an instant dislike to her, and was bitter towards her throughout the marriage. At twenty she had her first child, but he was regularly sick and after a few months he tragically died. Added to Kalinka's heartbreak was the atmosphere of anger and hate towards her. Far from supporting her in her grief, both husband and mother-in-law condemned her as an incompetent mother, responsible for the child's death. Soon after Kalinka was thrown out of their home.

When I listen to someone's story it is always my intention to listen to the Holy Spirit as well. Often I pray very quietly in tongues as I listen. It is as important for me to hear the Lord as the patient. The ulcers in Kalinka's stomach had started to develop soon after she had been thrown out. There was an obvious connection between the stress and heartbreak of her bereavement and divorce, and the ulcers. But why had they not gone after five years? And why had all the prayer for her, a believing Christian, had so little effect? Something was missing. We all sat quietly and prayed.

Into my thinking came an unexpected word: "curse". I felt confused and embarrassed. In over twenty years of praying with people this word had never cropped up before. Was this my imagination? It seemed such a foreign idea, more relevant to Bali than Bulgaria. There was only one way to find out…

"Katya" I said hesitantly, "does the word "curse" mean anything to you?"

"Oh, yes" was her immediate response, "we know of many stories in these mountain communities of someone being cursed. It is quite common here. If someone thinks himself or herself very badly wronged by someone else, they will seek revenge by going to the local witch and paying money for a curse on that person. Sometimes chickens are sacrificed. Many people here know about this."

What a sheltered life I enjoyed in North Derbyshire! It seemed unbelievable that such activities could be commonplace and common knowledge in modern day Europe; but, apparently, they were! Katya's reply both blessed and encouraged me. I spoke to Kalinka.

"Kalinka, I think you have some sort of curse on you, and that's why you've not been healed. How do you feel about that?"

Always, always I ask the patient for their gut feelings and response to whatever God appears to be revealing. It is impossible to pray without agreement, an agreement that comes by a unity in the Holy Spirit. Coerced or manipulated agreement bears no fruit, and can do much damage. What God reveals to one He has to reveal to all. Agreement should never be 'manufactured'; it must be genuine.

When I've asked for a response I always then pray quietly in tongues. God takes His time, and so should I.

To my surprise Kalinka didn't sideline the issue. " I think that might be right," she replied.

I was into something I had never experienced before. "Help, Lord" I prayed in my thoughts, "what do I do now?"

The key to much healing lies in the 'digging up' of the roots of a problem. I always think of the carrot as a good illustration of a problem to be prayed over. If one only pulls at the top some of the carrot breaks off, but the rest is left underground. Dig out the roots and you have the complete carrot. Similarly, the key to breaking curses is the exposing and removing of the roots. Pray only for the problem that is seen – the ulcers – and there may be temporary respite, but the problem is still rooted and will surface again.

Paul reminds us that when Jesus comes "He will bring to light what is hidden in darkness and will expose the motives of men's hearts." (I Cor. 4:5). It is this same Jesus who we can call upon to expose the problem we cannot see. After more prayer we all three came to the same agreement: the words and actions of Kalinka's Mother-in-Law five years earlier quite clearly pointed to her carrying out her threat to have Kalinka cursed.

The purpose of the Holy Spirit "bringing to light what is hidden in darkness" is not to condemn or judge others, but rather, in exposing their sin against us to bring forgiveness, reconciliation and healing. For Kalinka to be healed and set free, forgiveness was essential. It is through the Cross that we are healed (Isaiah 53:5). But what does that mean in practise? It means we have to forgive just as we receive forgiveness from God. Healing comes through an open, honest, and contrite heart that holds no grudges.

For Kalinka this forgiving of her Mother-in-Law had to be a 'thorough job'! It was not enough to merely repeat the words "I forgive you". It was important that the Holy Spirit helped Kalinka. So we prayed for the Holy Spirit to remind Kalinka of all the wickedness her Mother-in-Law had brought on her life...a refusal to love and accept her; a refusal to allow her to love her husband; a determination to bring enmity into the marriage relationship; the destruction of her confidence as wife and mother; the blaming of her for the child's death; the seeking out of witchcraft to curse her body and bring five years of misery and pain.

It was important that Kalinka's forgiveness was real, practical and absolutely unconditional.

But forgiveness does not stop there. We are dealing with a Holy God in whom there is no darkness at all. In the world's eye Kalinka is the innocent party. But in God's sight "all have sinned". So Kalinka also was required to repent of her wrongdoing in this relationship with her mother-in-law. Often I ask my patient to imagine the one they need to forgive sitting in front of them. I encourage them to speak forgiveness to them – "I forgive you for..." – and then to ask forgiveness from them... "Forgive me for..." This is not just a clever counselling technique. When the Holy Spirit is working in people's hearts this becomes reality. The captives are set free. The prisoners are released. It is a most beautiful thing. Repentance and forgiveness are at the heart of healing.

The same repentance and forgiveness was required of Kalinka towards her ex-husband. This Kalinka willingly and lovingly did. After this, it was my responsibility to pronounce and confirm what had taken place, forgiveness.

We can all encourage each other with God's promises. So when someone has repented and forgiven as deeply and as thoroughly as this, we should be ready to encourage them: "God has forgiven you"; "God has set you free"; "God has taken away your guilt"; "God has washed you clean". We all have a priestly calling to minister in this way in such circumstances. As Christians, whether male or female, we are members of "a

Royal Priesthood." (I Peter 2:9). The Bible never uses words just as pretty jargon! This is real, and behind it is a ministry we are called to exercise. When victims have been sucked into years of pain and guilt – often unjustly – it is the pronouncement by others that blesses them and encourages them. And encouragement they need. It is the confident stating by others that "God has forgiven you" that helps to rebuild faith and claim God's promises. This is the context of Jesus' words to His Disciples: "Receive the Holy Spirit. If you forgive anyone his sins, they are forgiven; if you do not forgive them, they are not forgiven." (John 20:23).

The words of prayer that I prayed over Kalinka were bold and strong and uncompromising:

" In the name of Jesus, Kalinka, I pronounce you forgiven of all your wrongdoing. In the Name of Jesus, Kalinka, I pronounce you free of all their wrongdoing on you. In the Name of Jesus, Kalinka, I break the curse put on you. I break its hold on your life and your body. I break the sickness in your body, and I pray, Lord Jesus, set Kalinka free, heal and restore her to full health."

It was only my first day in Troyan but the Lord was already beginning to teach me the difference between problems and symptoms. What had been Kalinka's problem? Everybody had naturally thought it was ulcers, and had, understandably, prayed for their removal. But the ulcers were simply the symptom. Kalinka's problem had been a curse. With the problem removed, we were all confident the symptoms would follow. Katya prayed a wonderful prayer over Kalinka. I never understood a word, but it still drove me to tears. After she finished we stayed silent a few minutes, bathing in the sunshine and in God's wonderful grace to save and to heal. It was a Heavenly moment.

Kalinka went back to her Ward a transformed person. A little while later she began to take food. Three hours later she was arranging her discharge for the following day. The next day her ulcers were completely gone. They never returned.

Before leaving the Hospital I was able to make an appointment to see the Hospital Director on the following day. With our driver still waiting for us, we returned to Katya's home. My commission from the Lord had been "to pray for them" and "to visit the Hospital." On my first morning in Troyan I began both assignments. I had hit the ground running. If I had needed any more assurance that I was where the Lord wanted me to be, I had it now!

Katya's father was waiting to greet me when we returned. Peter was a small, unassuming, and gentle man. He had returned from his fortnightly visit to the town prison. He eagerly took me on a tour round his small garden. He had chickens, and a small pen for a lamb, which he bought every spring. In front of the stairs draped the skeleton of the garden vine. (Many of the older folks who were fortunate enough to have gardens grew grapes.) Peter also had a 30-year old car – a battered East German Trabant—parked under cover next to the vine. It hadn't moved for years, but in Troyan nothing is wasted or thrown away.

I had expected Peter to ask many questions: what were my plans? How many times would I be visiting? Had I any ambitions for the Church? Had I got a plan or schedule to keep to? Instead he simply listened and joined in the conversation. He was a man who listens.

I was interested to know why Katya's English was so good. This was her story. A few years earlier some American missionaries had visited Troyan and made friends with Peter and his family. To return the hospitality, they invited Katya to America to study at Bible College. This she did for eighteen months before returning to Bulgaria. After eighteen months in the U.S. she had had the opportunity to stay on, study more and be employed by the Church. But she had declined the invitation, believing God always wanted her to serve the Church in Troyan. It had been a difficult and sacrificial decision. Here was the rarest of Saints – one who had chosen Bulgaria over the U.S.A! One of the blessings of her time in America had been the broadening of her understanding and experience of Church life. The experience would prepare her for our ministry in Troyan.

Having returned from the U.S.A. she met and married Vasil, who had recently left the Bulgarian army after joining at the remarkably young age of fourteen! He was a tall, strong man, with a gentle smile and eyes that betrayed experience beyond his years. His strength of character would prove to be a protection for Katya. With Vasil's approval, no one questioned the long hours that Katya spent with me in translation and prayer partnership.

Nanka announced lunch was ready. In the centre of the table was a whole fresh loaf of bread sliced by hand; each slice a full three centimetres thick! This, together with a bowl of homemade soup would fill us up until the evening meal.

Nanka loved her food and had great culinary skills. Her tiny kitchen comprised of a wood-burning stove with cooking plates on top, and a few metal pans. She and many like her had survived the lean times of the Stalin years by their own innovation and resourcefulness. Fruit and fruit juices would be stored in glass jars in the cellar. The fruit juices were made from the wild summer fruits of the woods, as well as raspberries and pears and apples from the garden. A tiny portion of cheap meat could produce faggots for nine people. These, together with the vegetables Peter grew in the tiny spaces available in the garden, provided an adequate and healthy meal. Every resource was used and everything had value.

From visiting many countries and sharing hospitality with poor people, I had learnt a few ground rules regarding meals. First and foremost: always accept whatever is put in front of you. The one exception for me had always been 'spicy'! So when travelling to India or Pakistan I always had to apologise ahead of the meal. In this way my apology was accepted and accommodated. To receive food and then say "I can't eat that" is the worst embarrassment and insult of all.

When food is put in front of you, forget about rules for how to use a fork or where to place the elbows. Of prime importance is to eat hungrily, pausing at intervals to say how delicious it all is. It is essential to show real enjoyment of what has been prepared for you. In many poor homes the family will go without for days to provide hospitality to strangers. Their reward is in seeing you lap it up!

After lunch Katya took me on a guided tour of the town. One striking feature were the large woodpiles outside almost every home. The wood was either purchased in the summer, or collected from the mountain forests with the appropriate permission and payment. Troyan was blessed indeed by this available and cheap supply of winter fuel. (As well as fuel and fruits, the forests also had abundant supplies of mushrooms, nuts and the occasional rabbit.) The winters in Bulgaria are cold and brutal. In the towns and villages out of reach of the mountains, winter mortality among the elderly is high.

Running through the centre of town was a large swelling river with two bridges spanning its banks. Between the bridges was a smart pedestrian walkway leading to the large open Town Square. Small cafes dotted one corner, with tables and chairs trespassing into the Square. It was an unusual sight for a February afternoon.

Proudly standing in the centre of the square was the eponymous stone monument incorporating the Hammer and Sickle. No one had bothered to take it down. The locals, familiar with it for half a century, had little to replace it with. The end of Communism in Bulgaria had been a two-edged sword. The first non-Communist government had been so corrupt and greedy at looting the nation's assets that after three years the nation voted the Communists back (in the guise of 'reformed' Socialists!'). Having learned how to steal under the banner of "post-Communist reconstruction", they proceeded to loot what little remained. The country became virtually bankrupt. It was a remarkable start to the beginning of what the Americans called "freedom". The town had been staring at this Stalinist monument for half a century, which boasted the laughable principles of justice and equality for all. But at least it had provided them with a job and a pension. Now they were "free" they had neither. .

By Western standards the town was unspoilt; no traffic; no pollution; no litter; no McDonalds or K.F.C. Who could afford fast food in a town where most struggled to find a scrap of meat to add to the soup? Troyan was unspoilt in 1998 because they had nothing to spoil it with!

THE THURSDAY EVENING MEETING

By teatime Pastor Peter's home was filling up. Angel, Peter's four-year-old grandson, was home from Nursery School and eager to learn all about the English stranger. He was a bright and happy little chap. His mother, Katya's sister, Valentina, introduced herself, as did her husband Krasimir. Krasimir had a steady job a few miles away. Jobs were hard to find in Troyan. During the Communist period there had been many state-owned factories, pumping out substandard goods no one wanted to buy. By contrast, the Post-Communist governments had promised economic change and prosperity; but nothing had happened. Now many of the younger men and women were looking further afield—to Greece, or Italy, or even better, England. The Mafia gladly obliged, with guaranteed packages of paperwork, jobs, accommodation, and contacts; and all for the first two year's pay! In desperation many were taking the offer.

The food was ready. Peter, as always, stood up and gave thanks. Homemade burgers, stuffed courgettes, soup and potatoes – and bread! Nanka placed two bottles of homemade fruit juice on the table. A special treat for us all.

Peter explained that the Church had an evening meeting every Thursday, and he would like me to preach. This came as a complete surprise. God had said nothing to me beforehand about preaching! I was equally surprised that Peter was willing to trust me with his pulpit on our first day of meeting. I reluctantly accepted. I had rarely preached in my Church at home.

There was little time to prepare anything, and nowhere to go to be quiet. So I excused myself a while before the meeting to walk the short distance to the tiny Church building. While slowly walking the streets I had a little argument with the Lord. "You never mentioned preaching" I grumbled. I was reminded that I was not on my own mission – but His. I was not there to do what I wanted, but to respond to the opportunities and situations that would open up for me. This was one of them. With no time to prepare a Bible message, I decided to simply share my story of what I was doing there.

The Church stood by the side of the river. It was the end section of a long two-storey building. It was difficult to put a date on it. One hundred years old? Two hundred years old? It was sad to see such lovely architecture suffering from fifty years of Communist neglect. By contrast, the end section used as a Church building had obviously been loved and cared for over the years. Inside there was a small raised stage at one end, a keyboard in the corner, and the traditional 'chapel chairs'. What marked it out from an English Chapel was the huge wood-burning stove temporarily constructed right in the centre of the room, with all the chairs surrounding it. In the spring the stove would be dismantled, but in the fiercest of winters, the Believers were comfortable. A basement had been constructed with a toilet for the children and small room for the kindergarten. The older children went outside to their Sunday School in another part of the long building. That was the part of the building concerning which I had first heard mention of the town of Troyan.

I sat at the front with Katya as my guide and translator. Unknown to me, instead of the usual twenty regulars, the Church filled up with perhaps fifty people. The Service was traditional with hymns and the occasional modern chorus, many of which I recognised and enjoyed singing in English. In every service Church tradition had created an interlude when anyone could stand up and make a prayer request or give a short testimony. Katya pointed to a lady speaking: "that's Kalinka's mother. She's explaining how you prayed for Kalinka. She's coming out of hospital tomorrow." It was the first news I had heard since the morning and was amazed how quickly she had recovered. Many others must have found out beforehand, decided to come and see for themselves. The entire Church appeared to know of my visit. News travels fast in Troyan!

After another hymn Peter gestured for me to take the rostrum.

"Slavalaboga!" I said, half grunting and half roaring!

This Bulgarian word translates something like 'nice to meet you'. It is a traditional Bulgarian greeting. Everybody relaxed and started smiling. I relaxed also, and decided to tell them a joke. This concerned the Bulgarian 'yes' and 'no'. The Bulgarian for yes is "Da", but it is said with the head shaking from side to side, as if expressing 'no'. Likewise the Bulgarian for 'no' is "Ne", but is said with the head nodding, as if expressing 'yes'. (Outside of India I had never experienced head movement with language.) I explained how confused I was – when I said "Da" I instinctively nodded, saying "Ne"; but when I said "Ne" I instinctively shook my head, saying "Da". I then circled my head in a spin, indicating how confused I was! Everyone laughed and enjoyed the joke. Like Northern people, Bulgarians love a joke about themselves.

I introduced myself, and explained how the Lord had brought me to Troyan; how the call of the Lord was confirmed by five brothers and sisters in my home Church; and how I had arrived – as if landing from outer space – on Pastor Peter's doorstep that very morning. As I spoke I began to see eyes filling up, just as Katya and Nanka's had. The enormity of what God had done in one day was getting to me also. I was filling up too!

I finished and sat down. Peter spoke after me, and although I couldn't understand him, I kept hearing " Pastor Allan". I realized I had been promoted to "Pastor". At home I wasn't in Church leadership, so I wondered how such a title would go down in England! But in Troyan it was never a problem. Some called me "Pastor" and some called me "Brother". But the children somehow knew best: they simply called me "Allan".

I knew in my spirit that Peter was affirming all I had said. He was indeed a godly man. In the four years of visiting Troyan, Pastor Peter had not always understood what was going on, but he recognized the hand of God in the healed and changed lives of those we prayed with. No doubt he had many quiet conversations with his daughter to keep him on track. He knew God was at the heart of what was happening. He was the most wonderfully humble man, who gave himself completely for the Church and the Gospel. He was delighted to see me in Troyan; and his support gave an important blessing on the four-year ministry that would follow. I will always be grateful for his friendship and support.

Chapter Two

BULGARIAN HOSPITALITY

The evening meeting came to a close. Pastor Peter beckoned me, in the traditional manner, to follow him to the Church door so as to greet everyone as they left. Everyone greeted me in turn. "Slavalaboga!" There were handshakes, and a few enthusiastic bear hugs. When all seemed to be finished we re-entered the building. To my astonishment there were still around twelve people patiently waiting to see me. This was the first of what I can only describe as my 'surgeries': people who would wait to see me after each meeting. The surgeries continued for four and a half years.

My wife is a doctor and deals with 'surgeries' every day. She is allocated around ten minutes a patient to try and diagnose their real problem. Often patients present a less important problem, only mentioning the real reason they are there as they leave. A doctor has to be sensitive to this and pick up the key words spoken that indicate a problem. Some patients come for little more than comfort or reassurance, and are presented with placebos – harmless pills that the patient believes will help. Some patients need specialist help and counselling. Many times decisions cannot be made without X-ray information.

My 'surgeries' were soon structured on similar principles. People came to see me for many reasons. Some simply wanted a prayer of blessing or reassurance. Others wanted help for jobs or visas. Others presented what appeared a simple problem, for example, back pain; but it quickly became clear that the problem was more complex and needed more time and questions. Some needed a 'spiritual X-ray', as we shall see later.

On my first evening meeting I was presented with a queue. I remember clearly that first young man who asked for my help. Katya and I sat with him privately in one corner of the building. He was in his early twenties. He had come regularly to Church for a long time, but in the previous few months had

had a disturbing experience. Whenever he started walking to Church, he found himself physically halted. He couldn't move forward. I had never heard or read of such a thing. Katya knew the young man and confirmed his story. I asked him if something had happened around the time this strange experience first began.

"I cut off the engagement with my fiancé. There were terrible rows, and my girl friend's mother threatened revenge."

To my utter amazement it seemed like another curse!

The young man remembered the argument clearly. He had been at his fiancée's home, explaining why he had stopped the engagement. When he went to leave he noticed a button missing from his coat. He didn't think anything about it at the time, but now realised his girl friend's mother had stolen the button.

"Why should she do this?" I asked Katya.

"Oh," she said, "it's often done in witchcraft. They are asked to bring something – anything—belonging to the person who is to be cursed. They believe it makes the magic more powerful."

Because his girlfriend was not a Christian and refused any contact with the Church, he had finished with her. So her mother had arranged a curse on him in revenge, which would cut him off from the Church he loved.

Katya and I found ourselves praying in the same manner that we had with Kalinka that same morning. Had this young man heard of how we prayed with Kalinka? It seemed a strange coincidence. As with Kalinka his heart was also open to the Lord to forgive and to repent. He held nothing back, and in the name of Jesus the curse was broken. With Pastor Peter participating, we then prayed for healing and renewal in his life.

The prayer time with him had taken about forty minutes, and there were still about ten people patiently but persistently waiting to be seen. I asked each in turn for a brief description of their need. Silently I appealed to the Lord for Wisdom. The Bible gives a special promise regarding Wisdom – it's available on tap!

"If any of you lacks wisdom, he should ask God, who gives generously to all without finding fault, and it will be given to him." (James 1:5)

We prayed for one or two immediately, but most were earmarked for later. We found it necessary to make appointments for the Friday and Saturday. Having asked for Wisdom, I went on 'instinct' in deciding who needed more time. In prayer situations such as these gut instincts and the leading of the Holy Spirit merge together!

Finally I was free to walk into the cool evening air. Katya was still translating. She motioned to a lady with two girls: "They want to invite you for an evening meal tomorrow." "OK" I said, putting them on the list. Still another lady was waiting to see me. "This is Bojana", Katya explained, "she heard that you were staying in that awful hotel. She would like to invite you to stay with her and her grandson. It's more comfortable. You can go tonight." I accepted gratefully and without hesitation.

I said "goodnight" to Vasil and Katya, thanking them for being so patient. Ivan, Bojana's grandson, stayed behind to help. We walked the short distance to my hotel, collected my small case, and checked out.

BOJANA

Bojana's home was a comfortable upmarket ground floor flat in a small block built before the Communist period. The flat was well furnished with quality curtains and carpets, good furniture, and a rare upright piano in fine working order. Bojana lived with her grandson, Ivan, a tall, dark and handsome seventeen year old student in the sixth form at the local High School.

Behind the appearance of easy-living comfort hid Bojana and Ivan's tragic story. Bojana's daughter, her only child, had been a first class student and qualified as a doctor. She then married an airline pilot. For Bulgaria, and especially in the austere Communist times, such a union of talent and promise was a 'dream ticket'.

After five years of marriage and a little four-year old boy, tragedy struck. While her husband was frequently away with his work, Bojana's daughter had an affair. Inevitably her husband found out. He was so heart-broken by her betrayal that he took his own life. Bojana's daughter never recovered from her grief and guilt, and six months after his death she also committed suicide. Ivan, their little boy, was left an orphan, and Bojana brought him up.

There was nothing in Ivan's seventeen-year old demeanour that hinted at his tragic loss. He was highly gifted, polite, gentle and mature beyond his years. Bojana had done an excellent job.

Bojana herself was a retired pastry chef. Her skills were outstanding. She took every opportunity to make me the most delicious breads, cakes and pastries. Breakfast in particular was always a feast, surrounded as I was by twice what I could eat. Fortunately I have a love of bread and pastries, and this eased the stress of the daily search for extra capacity! Bojana would make sure of that. She would sit opposite me at the breakfast table and insist I over-indulged myself. (Bulgarians are not subtle in either their eating or drinking). Any hint of dissension was countered by a threatening look of disapproval. She was delighted at this unexpected opportunity to use her skills again; and we somehow learnt to compromise with each other.

Bojana became my Bed and Breakfast 'Landlady'. I had a key and was welcome to come and go as I pleased. She never complained at the late times I often arrived in the evening. The men in Troyan had a routine of being out all day – even when they had no job! But by six or seven in the evening they always returned. There were no pubs or clubs, and I never saw one drunk all the time I visited Troyan. I was quickly aware of how unusual it was to be coming in at ten and even eleven o'clock at night. But Bojana never once complained. Nor did she ever ask or hint of payment. Her hospitality was free, generous and genuine. She treated me like a son, without any thought of reward.

The following day I had arranged to visit Peter's home at 9.00a.m. Katya and I had a full day's programme ahead of us, and most evenings we would be invited to someone's home for a meal. At times we had to refuse the offers. First, there were too many people who needed prayer, and second, there was a risk of neglecting Katya's parents' hospitality. To avoid this last problem it became routine that the first evening of every visit to Troyan would be spent at Pastor Peter's home.

But on that first Friday and Saturday evening in Troyan I was given hospitality by some special people.

KALINKA'S PARENTS

Kalinka's parents had greeted me on the Thursday evening with heartfelt gratitude, and immediately invited me to their home the following night. They were long-standing members of the Church and had known Katya since her childhood.

Their apartment block was of typical Communist construction: cold and boring. Individuality, even expressed in architecture, was always suspiciously seen as an Imperialist influence on Socialist thinking. Even in art and architecture conformity was the rule. So every Communist-built apartment block in Troyan was exactly like all the others, the only distinguishing marks being the numbers on the main entrance doors. All over Eastern Europe in the 50's and 60's the Communists organised mass movements of people out of the countryside and into the towns and cities. The object was the control of the masses together with the building of industrial economies. To provide for this, large numbers of tenement blocks were hastily constructed. In each would be appointed families responsible for alerting the authorities to any suspicious or illegal activity. Spies and informers were everywhere. In Troyan, as in other towns, vacated and uninhabitable homes were handed to the romanies, who were forced out of their nomadic lifestyle and into small settled communities.

We arrived at the inadequately lit entrance. The dank concrete steps led to four brown wooden doors on each floor. Katya rang the bell and we entered a warm and comfortable apartment. Kalinka's father was a well warn, big-hearted Bulgarian. Obviously grateful for what had happened, he met me with a vice-like handshake and hug, scouring my cheek with his high tensile whiskers!

One small round dining table in the corner of the room was already half full with food. We sat down, gave thanks, and began to eat. Kalinka's mother disappeared during the conversation and more food arrived. Followed by more...and more... Salad... chicken... sausage... mutton... It just kept on coming! I never experienced hunger in Bulgaria.

DONKA

Our invitation on the Saturday was to a very different home. Instead of a Soviet-style apartment block we were outside a small courtyard at the centre of a row of much older housing – perhaps two hundred years old – near the centre of town. The huge wooden double door might well have been original. Its large semi-circular top was enclosed in an equally imposing stone archway. Perhaps there had been a livery and stables here at some time. A tiny entrance door was built into the great door. Having rung the bell for attention, Donka quickly let us in. We walked across a small courtyard into the hallway of the building.

Donka was a jolly, plump lady in her late thirties. She was a gypsy, but had married a non-gypsy Bulgarian. The distinction was not at first apparent to me. In England, the class system is largely an historical anachronism. But in Bulgaria there are very clearly defined unofficial classes within the population. The Bulgarians are a mix of Balkan Slavs from the West and Greeks from the South. Added to these are the second-class citizens – the Turks from the North. The cultural distinction is in their religions. While the Slavs and Greeks are Orthodox Christians, the Turks are Muslim. These two groups – Orthodox and Muslim – have fought wars in Eastern Europe for over a thousand years. At the centre of this historical dispute was the 'Vatican' of Orthodox Christianity, namely, Constantinople, which was invaded and taken over by the Muslims. The "Blue Mosque" now in the centre of Istanbul (Constantinople) is the extended and refurbished 'Vatican' Cathedral of the Orthodox world. ("Vatican" is a deliberate description since the old city of Constantinople was home to the Orthodox 'Pope', a patron as influential and powerful as his Catholic counterpart is today.) Because of this history it is not surprising that Muslim Turks are regarded as second-class citizens in Bulgaria.

But even lower down the social order are the gypsies. These have their origins in either the Balkans (Christian Gypsies) or Turkey (Muslim Gypsies). Although mixing freely for business, their small communities are defined by their religious culture. Every gypsy belongs in one of these communities – unless she marries a Bulgarian. That is what Donka had done.

In the Hallway Donka's two children; Mariya, a bright twelve years old, and Eva, a shy ten year old, greeted us. We removed our shoes and entered their tiny home. Taking up half the room was an ancient double bed. This left little space for the wardrobe with a black and white TV on top. A small makeshift dining table had been placed by the side of the bed so that two of us could sit on the bed. This allowed us all to get around the table to eat. This room was their only room! It was their home, in which the three of them had to sleep, eat, play, do homework, bring friends, take care of their clothes and… survive. There was a tiny kitchen on the other side of the Hall for their use, plus an outside shared toilet in the yard in which they somehow washed.

The girls' father was a builder. Finding no work around Troyan, he had gone to Greece where even subsistence wages were better than those in Bulgaria. He must have had little choice, faced with the sleeping arrangements for his family. The way this family rose above their circumstances moved me deeply. The girls were clean and well clothed. There was no indication from their looks or manner that they had to tolerate such deprivation. They had stood outside the Church on Thursday for an hour simply to invite me for supper. I was deeply humbled.

Mariya and Eva were both gifted children. Twelve-year-old Mariya was already teaching in the Sunday School. Eva was a talented cook. Together they had spent most of the day preparing the meal. It would soon be apparent they had also spent all they had on the food. But it was such a blessing to receive and enjoy Donka's hospitality. In the centre of the table proudly stood a two-litre bottle of Coca-Cola (the genuine article). For a family of three living on £5-50p per week, this was champagne indeed. The food came in from the kitchen with the anticipation of the Lord Mayor of London's Banquet.

I was asked to give thanks. I searched for words that rose above the jargon. How do you say "thank you" when three people who have nothing give you everything they have?

"Lord, we want to thank you tonight because you are so wonderful and faithful to us. We want to thank you tonight because you love us and take care of us and provide for our every need. We want to thank you tonight for this delicious food and for the love and care with which is has been prepared. As you fill our bodies, fill also our hearts with your love and grace. Amen."

I was moved to tears, as I still am when remembering it. That poor people could live in such impossible circumstances, and yet smile and laugh. What a wonderful role model Mariya was for the younger children in the Church. We tucked in, enjoying and appreciating everything before us.

The hospitality of Donka and her children was so beautiful that I tried to bring everyone who came from England to experience it. Without exception they were deeply moved by the experience. Without realizing it, these three were ministering great blessing to Christians from England. They were feasting at a banqueting table beyond this world.

At the end of the evening I returned to my Bed and Breakfast. To my dismay I discovered that Bojana had also spent the day preparing food. She had utilized her incredible skills to produce the most amazing pastries. If a missionary needs the grace to survive with little food or the wrong type of food, then he or she also needs grace from above to enjoy a hearty meal when already full!

After that, each morning I would make a point of asking Bojana not to cook supper, as it would be provided elsewhere.

Chapter Three

MY FIRST SUNDAY

Arranging this first visit to Troyan had presented me with a difficulty: how long should I go for? It wasn't like arranging a short break in Blackpool, where one could cancel and return home if the weather turned. I had to book flights, and the flight schedule determined how many days I would be 'stuck' in Bulgaria. There were many things that could go wrong. I might have the wrong address. The Pastor might have moved, or been away for some reason. The Pastor might have had no one to translate.

Faced with these uncertainties, I had booked my flights from Tuesday to Monday. This plan allowed a few days in Troyan before the Sunday. If the very worst had happened and I had found no one, then at least I could have met with some Christians on the Sunday. That had been my thinking. But God had planned it differently: namely, that I should meet with the Church before the Sunday Service!

Now, on this first Sunday morning they were not only coming to meet me, but also to hear me. Pastor Peter had again invited me to preach at both the morning and evening services. I needed help. Although I had been a Church of England Minister for ten years, the work of full-time ministry was a long time in the past. I had left the parochial ministry in 1982. Even the title "Pastor" that I was being given seemed inappropriate. I had tried to refuse the title, claiming I was just a small businessman (which I am). The protest fell on deaf ears.

I decided that my two Sunday Sermons would be simple and straightforward talks on the two foundation stones of the Christian Life: namely, Conversion and Baptism in the Holy Spirit. These subjects were of personal importance in my own experience, even more so because of the unusual way it had all happened.

I had decided to be ordained at the young age of sixteen. After studying Theology at Nottingham University I had then gone to Wells Theological College in Somerset before being ordained in 1972. From my R.I. studies in the sixth form onwards I had become a liberal theologian. A 'liberal' theologian might be described as one who knows more about what he doesn't believe than what he does! Nottingham increased the intensity with which I questioned and challenged Biblical teaching, and my Church of England Theological Training did nothing to bring it all together again. They were as lost as I was; lost in a sea of biblical criticism. It was a classic case of the blind leading the blind! I served as Curate in Castleford and then moved to Howden Minster near Goole in Yorkshire.

I arrived at this prestigious parish in the summer of 1974. The Vicar, a certain Canon Graham, was high up in Church circles, on the General Synod (the Church Parliament) and an important official in the Diocese of York. He was a man of great experience and influence. He taught me how to visit efficiently. He taught me how to persuade newcomers to get involved in Church life. He taught me how to make the most of my time; and for the first six months in Howden he was an inspiration.

But in the following March, two things happened that would change my life forever. The first was a picture that God put in my imagination. It was of the variety entertainer spinning plates on the top of wooden sticks. The very clever ones could keep up to 100 plates spinning without falling. God showed me that my ministry was like the plate-spinners – constantly keeping people motivated to go to Church by my own skill and effort.. If I was good I could do 60 or 80. If I was brilliant, perhaps 100. And then God spoke into my thoughts with a question I have never forgotten; **"Allan, do you want to spend your life spinning plates?"** I knew the answer was "no".

The second strange thing that happened in March 1975 occurred during one of the mid-week Lenten meetings the Church traditionally held. There was a speaker I had never seen before, the Rev. Bertie Keenan. He was a Vicar from a parish not far away; a Protestant (I was 'High Church'!) with a strong Irish accent. I listened to his talk intently, but it was not what he was saying but who he was that focussed my attention. I knew this man had something special, and whatever it was, I wanted it too. A week later I arranged to visit him at his home.

"Arrrr my boy!" he said, in his thick Irish accent, "The Lord has a plan for you, He has great things for you. But first you have to be built up spiritually." I was all ears. The fruits of six years of theological study were now cast aside. This man had answers.

"You've got to ask Jesus into your heart and life. Are you ready to do that?"

I was. He spoke of the need for repentance, and to come unconditionally to the Cross. Then he led me in a short and simple prayer of faith:

"Lord Jesus, I believe that you died for me on the Cross. I ask you to forgive all my wrongdoing and unbelief. Please come into my heart and life, as my Saviour and Friend; and live with me forever. Amen."

Afterwards he gave me a little booklet explaining very simply with little pictures what I had done. I left knowing God was in all that was happening. Over the next two weeks God spoke to me again; "You must be Baptised in the Holy Spirit." I telephoned Bertie again and went to see him.

"Arrrrr my boy" he greeted me, this time with his wife.

I explained that I wanted to be Baptised in the Holy Spirit. I had little idea what this was, but whatever it was God wanted me to have it, and so did I!

"Arrrrr my boy, that's great. Praise the Lord!"

Bertie explained how we needed to be empty in order to be filled. To empty our lives of 'spiritual' involvements that were contrary to the Holy Spirit. Again I repented of past involvement with fortune telling, Astrology, superstitions and anything else I could think of. Then Bertie and his wife both laid hands on my head and shoulders and prayed for me to be filled with the Holy Spirit They continued praying in tongues for about five minutes. After that I left for home, and in the car on the way back began to sing in tongues...

I had become a Christian and been Baptised in the Holy Spirit. And that was my new testimony – however inconvenient the theology might be for those who heard it! This conversion, for that is what it was, brought me immediately into both strong acceptance and vitriolic rejection.

I was immediately accepted by one of the family doctors in the parish, Dr. Andrew Williamson. Andrew was a mature Christian and older than me. God was about to use his wisdom and counsel to protect and encourage me during the difficult times ahead.

The rejection came, to my surprise, from my own Vicar, who was almost paranoid in his hatred of Charismatic Christianity. He spent every Monday morning for the next eighteen months grilling and interrogating me, intent on finding some heretical statement from me as a ruse for my dismissal. Many times he tried to persuade me to abandon my testimony of conversion, or at least tone it down. This I refused. If the language was good enough for Jesus it was good enough for me. It was a personal insult to him that after 3 years as priest and preacher of the Gospel, I had now become a Christian. Sadly, we were never reconciled.

Now, 23 years later, I was preparing two talks for the Believers in Troyan: The morning talk would explain Jesus' instruction to the theologian Nicodemus – "you must be Born Again" (John 3:7); and the evening talk would be a simple explanation of Paul's question to the Ephesians – "Did you receive the Holy Spirit when you believed?" (Acts 19:2). These two talks would be a reminder of the foundations on which we build. They would also present my own 'spiritual credentials' to the leadership of the Church.

The services all had the same pattern. As on the Thursday evening, a number stood up and publicly declared how God had answered their prayers and healed them. Testimonies to the Grace of God to heal and save are a mighty weapon in convicting the world that Jesus is alive. Even in a tiny Church community like this word gets around. Holy Gossip is a powerful tool in spreading the Gospel.

After the meetings the people just wouldn't go home. There was always a small crowd patiently waiting with requests. "Help, Lord" I would secretly pray, "I need your knowledge and wisdom. Show me what needs more time." Before I became a Christian I thought that Christian ministry was about trying to be as Christ-like as possible; attempting to follow His example. But after my conversion I realised that was a distortion of what the New Testament teaches. Trying to be like Jesus is both futile and impossible… and exhausting too! It is no longer about me trying to be like Jesus, but allowing the Lord Jesus to live through me. It is about calling on the Holy Spirit to give me Jesus' mind, Jesus' thoughts, Jesus' feelings, Jesus' understanding, Jesus' words, and Jesus' actions. In short, it is Jesus' Ministry and not my own. Paul described it like this: "I no longer live, but Christ lives in me." (Galatians 2:20). Far from trying to be like Him, I have to get out of the way! I have to decrease so that He can increase (John 3:30).

I needed God's wisdom with everyone who came for help after the Services, and God gave generously. The people were complete strangers to me, with an unintelligent language, and a foreign culture. Only God could look down and see what was needed. I was totally reliant on His knowledge and wisdom.

In trusting this wisdom I often made surprising decisions. I would arrange two hours to someone who had an apparently 'straightforward' prayer need. There are many Church meetings today when an invitation for prayer is made, but only a few minutes of prayer is on offer—where time is not available beyond the confines of the meeting. Sometimes people step forward in a courageous 'last ditch' appeal for help. Without wisdom from those who minister, opportunities are lost. With some problems Jesus needs time.

Katya and I never knew in advance what prayer requests would be coming to us. We had everything from headaches to cancers, jobs to visas. At times I felt quite uncomfortable that what was coming to me could easily be prayed for among friends. But it was important to take every request seriously.

PESHKA

Peshka was the Church Caretaker. A quiet middle-aged widow who held the key to the building, she faithfully cared for it as well as opening and locking the place at every meeting. She would patiently wait for us all to disperse after every Service.

Many of the people who shared their problems were quite open and loud with what they had to share. (Wherever possible I tried to create privacy, but not everyone needed or wanted it). So Peshka heard many of the problems and prayers. She never complained at the extra hours every week. Instead Katya and I were treated to her generous hospitality.

Peshka's only Son had successfully migrated to the U.S.A. and it was her heart's desire to join him. Her very first request to me was that I 'get her a Visa' to go to the States. I gently explained that I couldn't do that, but I knew a Man who could – Jesus. We called all those around her to come together in a circle and we prayed for the Visa.

On another occasion she quietly came up to Katya after the Sunday morning Service. She had what is commonly called a "Frozen Shoulder" – and could not raise her right arm above her shoulder. I was fortunate that this happened on a visit when Dr. Andrew was accompanying me. A medical diagnosis of physical illness before prayer is always helpful, and sometimes essential. The more specific prayer is, the most powerful it is. So Andrew briefly examined her arm, knowing exactly what to touch and what questions to ask.

We stood in a small circle, with Pastor Peter joining us, and bowed our heads to pray. "O Lord, what do we do?" I silently prayed. I was learning fast that the obvious response what not always the right one. Surely it was just a case of asking Jesus to heal her shoulder? But the Bible says: "Trust in the Lord with all your heart and lean not on your own understanding."(Proverbs 3:5). The word the Lord gave me I shared quietly with Andrew: "Ask her to lift up her arms and praise the Lord." It seemed at odds with the fact she couldn't lift her right arm above her shoulder! Nevertheless, Andrew responded. In the reassuring way that doctors have, he said to her: "we're just going to pray in the Spirit, and as we do I want you to gently lift your arms in the air. I'll help you." With that we all started to pray and praise the Lord. As we did so, Andrew kept gently lifting her arms until they were both straight above her head! Peshka's face beamed with delight. We then prayed for the muscles to be fully restored, and for the Holy Spirit to fill her heart and soul. It was the first time I had seen her 'in the Spirit' like that. If she had been unsure about the Baptism of the Holy Spirit before, she was never unsure again.

Six months before my final departure from Troyan Peshka came to see me with the exciting news that she had been granted a Residence Visa in the United States.

We are told that one of the Disciples asked Jesus: "teach us to pray."(Luke 11:1). This simple request hints at a whole host of teaching that Jesus gave to His Disciples which we have no record of, except for the Lord's Prayer. For example, we have no record of His teaching them to cast out demons. But it is clear that Jesus' teaching to his disciples was on-going, and involved them being sent out to practise what He had taught them.(see Luke 10:1-12). After the theory came the practical. Gradually their understanding and confidence matured until they could rejoice that "even the demons submit to us in your name." (Luke 10:17).

The request, "teach us to pray", was as much about the 'what' as about the 'how'. *What* do I pray for in these circumstances, or when faced with this problem? Their confusion was understandable. For example, they had been with the Lord when the paralytic had been presented to him. Faced with a man who couldn't walk, Jesus addressed the man's *guilt problem* first! When presented with a desperate problem of paralysis, he forgave the man's sins (Mark 2:5).

They had seen Jesus deliver an out-of control evil spirit by commanding "be quiet", and then "come out of him"(Mark 1:25). To the leper Jesus had spoken only two words: "be clean!"(Mark 1:41). The disciples *must* have asked Jesus to " teach us *what* to pray" as well as how to pray. We usually know how to pray, but often stumble with *what* to pray for.

Traditional ways of praying and professional counselling techniques, while sometimes of help, can also be a barrier to effective prayer if we depend on them rather than the Holy Spirit. Our own insight and understanding can get in the way of effective prayer. We instinctively ask ladies to pray with ladies and men to pray with men. We sometimes forget the God-given partnership that men and women have in Jesus to counsel and to pray. Two women praying for a woman can create over-empathy; similarly two men praying for a men can be threatening and overbearing. We need the Holy Spirit to help us not only with how and what to pray, but also who to pray with. Political correctness should never be our criteria.

On that first Sunday in Troyan some of the many prayer requests could not be carried out. We had run out of time. So Katya and I produced a list of people we promised to visit when I next returned to Troyan. I had little alternative but to return. It was also a reassurance that God wanted me back.

After the Sunday evening service came the gifts. Someone baked a cake for my wife. Another had a small clay bowl made locally. There were other trinkets, each one given with love and appreciation. And what do you give when you are a gypsy child and have nothing? Well, you go into the field (or someone's garden!) and collect a few flowers, and wrap the stalks in tin foil.

Chapter Four

MY SECOND VISIT.

I returned to England with mixed feelings. I was overjoyed to witness the many blessings the Lord had done in people 's lives. I was also encouraged that I had heard the Lord correctly concerning going to Troyan. All the doors had opened for me, and I couldn't wait to share the news with family and Church.

However my joy was tempered with confusion. My few days in Troyan had raised as many questions as it had answered. What sort of a commitment was I getting into? Would this be two or three visits or twenty-three visits? How should my Church be involved? Didn't the Lord send missionaries out in two's and not one's? In time I would call on my long-time prayer partner Dr. Andrew. I would also bring over Church elders to 'see what was going on'. But I never found anyone in my Church with the same heart burden that I had to go and pray with these people.

Sooner or later I knew the question would be asked: "why are you going and what exactly are you aiming to achieve?" I would have liked to have had a satisfying answer ready for this question, but I never found one. A door had opened and people were waiting for my return visit. They were queuing at the door. I was going because... ... I couldn't *not* go.

The members of my small Pentecostal Church were delighted at what had happened; but they were also bewildered. Breaking curses? Where has all this come from? A small number had a similar doctrinal background to the older Church members in Troyan. For them it was impossible that a Spirit-filled Born-again believer could ever be demonised or come under a curse. What had happened in Troyan was now challenging some long and tightly held beliefs in my Church. I was 'rocking the boat' a little but I couldn't do anything about it!

There was no way I could start to 'pick and choose' which healings I should share with them. So the testimony of the healings in Troyan was for a few a double-edged sword.

Within weeks I had booked my return flights to Bulgaria. With freezing winters that made Troyan almost inaccessible, and summers in the 40's, I decided October would be a good month to return. I was amazed that the Troyan Christians were prepared to wait six months until my next visit; but most did. Some of their problems, spiritual as well as physical, they had carried for years. But I must not give the impression that they were incapable of praying for themselves and receiving healing and blessing. Of course they were. What I was being presented with, especially in the early years, were problems that went much deeper. They had searched for answers but found none.

I was much more prepared for my second visit, and this time established a programme of travel which I would keep to for most of my visits: travelling out on a Wednesday and returning the following Monday.

Now I was able to give full preparation to my talks in the meetings. It became an established pattern that I would preach at each of the three meetings on every visit. I had returned to England with a deep compassion for these Bulgarian believers, and I wanted to encourage them. I found in my thoughts a simple but beautiful message. "God loves you, God cares for you, and God wants to bless you." I learnt these words in Bulgarian, and often shared them in the meetings. Their response was always delightful to see. Their faces lit up, with shouts of "Amen" and "Hallelujiah".

As I prepared my talks for the Church meetings I thought much about what these Bulgarian believers had been through. They had been invaded first by the Nazis and then by Soviet Russia. For 45 years they had been governed by Moscow. Their identity and pride had been suppressed into Communist conformity. Their ancient culture was now infested with injustice and corruption, the classic fruits of Communist rule! Above all that, they were a people forgotten and largely ignored by the West, a people seemingly no use to anybody.

Troyan not only suffered from these nation-wide feelings of deprivation and abandonment, but it was also an insignificant town of no strategic or financial value to the State – and in the middle of nowhere. For most the only hope seemed to be an illegal (and extremely expensive) ticket to find work in Greece or the West. For the older ones there seemed no hope. Troyan had no future. Its industry and economy was bankrupt.

The believers had suffered more than most. Communist governments are masters at creating suspicion and intrigue among believers. In the West we have no understanding of this ploy. The Communist mantra had always been: "if we can't destroy them we'll divide them, and watch them destroy themselves". Many of the believers had paid heavily, losing jobs, education, homes and husbands. One Troyan believer died in prison under interrogation. Even after the fall of Communism, suspicion and mistrust of Evangelical Christianity is kept alive by repeated denouncements on Bulgarian TV: "Evangelicals and Pentecostals are the same as Mormons and Jehovah's Witnesses; they are *all* non-Christian Sects. Only the Orthodox Church holds the true Christian faith."

But God's Word to them was heartening and encouraging: "God loves you, God cares for you, and God wants to bless you."

FOUR MIRACLES

A small crowd waited to see me after the Thursday evening meeting. More than half were prayed for on the spot. Whenever possible we involved other believers around us, including teenagers, in this ministry. I would take every opportunity I could to show that what we were doing was neither magical nor mysterious. Sometimes I would encourage the person who asked for prayer to pray themselves, with all around saying the "Amen".

There were some occasions when requests were turned down, but the believers were still encouraged because we prayed for other things. This happened a number of times with the elderly asking for their aches and pains to disappear. "I want the body of a 20 year old also!" I would joke. What they needed was to draw closer to God and know His love and security. They would always go away encouraged and blessed after such a prayer.

One elderly lady, Gelyazka, whom Katya knew very well, requested we visit her home. Her son and daughter-in-law and their two small children lived with her, and one of the children was sick.

As we walked the short distance from the centre of town to her apartment, Katya told me Gelyazka's story. She had been brought up a believer, but had married an unbeliever. This arrangement was not uncommon because there were three Christian young women for every Christian young man! But such marriages are invariably problematic. Wives pray for their husbands to become a Christian, often preaching and even nagging them. Husbands find even the most discreet wives' commitment to Church and fellowship an embarrassment and threat. In Bulgaria especially, the shame on an unbeliever having an Evangelical wife can bring hostility from both family and friends.

Eventually her husband could take it no more. He gave her an ultimatum: "leave the Church or leave me!" Bravely, she refused to leave her Church. As a result she was thrown out of home, and cut off from both husband and children.

In the Communist days such tragedies were not uncommon. Its Atheistic system naturally supported the unbelieving partner. There was no recourse to law when Pentecostal believers were suspected of Western collaboration. The local government had little sympathy with women with such 'extremist' religious convictions. They were fanatics; and the children would be better off without them!

Gelyazka had paid a heavy price for standing up for Jesus; but her faith and love for the Lord remained beautiful, simple and steadfast.

We entered her tiny apartment, and found ourselves in a home full of chaos. Baby Cots seemed to be everywhere, and the place was littered with baby clothes, nappies, bottles etc. One thing immediately caught my eyes. On the old pre-war sideboard proudly stood a brand new, state of the art 28" colour TV. It was linked by satellite to programmes all over Europe – including the BBC. This was the son-in-law's pride and joy and he alone had the right to turn it off!

This modern and expensive high-tech equipment seemed so out of place among all the old and worn out furniture and carpets. But I had to remind myself that the Bulgarians had been deprived of all access to the West for half a century. They were too poor to travel, and few Westerners ever bothered to visit Troyan. Two generations had been completely cut off from the outside world; and now, suddenly, Satellite TV was available. Who was I to criticise them spending their life savings on such things?

Having had a tour of the Satellite Dish and its myriad of programmes, the TV was finally switched off! As if in protest, the baby began to cry. The daughter-in-law looked stressed and tired. The little family had all to share the same bedroom. Her lack of sleep was understandable.

I cannot now remember what the problem was with the little boy, but by the morning it had gone.

Nor was this Gelyazka's only request during my visits to Troyan. The next was made again outside the Church after an evening Service. She did not have good eyesight, but now she had lost completely the sight in her left eye! Katya knew Gelyazka was a solid Christian and not simply attention-seeking. The problem was real. She spoke very quietly and without emotion to Katya. So right there—in the street—we laid hands on her, and claimed her healing in the name of Jesus. After we finished, to my amazement, she calmly announced: "it's OK now". Her sight had been restored. Saints like her, whose lives have been pruned and refined, don't need a lot of fuss. A few words are all that is needed.

A year or so after this we were again invited to Gelyazka's home to pray for one of the grandchildren. Dr. Andrew was accompanying me on this visit. Little had changed from my first visit: the TV, the chaos, the cots and baby clothes etc. But now there was another baby, and the daughter-in-law appeared more exhausted than ever. We had nearly finished and were about to depart when Gelyazka indicated she had something to tell us. This time, whatever it was, it was private. She didn't want anyone to hear, not even her daughter-in-law. She took advantage of her daughter-in-law being temporarily out of the room putting the baby to bed, to quietly inform us she had just been diagnosed at the Hospital with cancer. Could we pray for her?

My heart sank. I felt uneasy under this pressure. We could only whisper, and we only had minutes. We couldn't pray aloud. All my routine of waiting on the Holy Spirit for help was thrown out of the window! We had little alternative but to get on with it! "Lord Jesus, please take away this Cancer. Heal and restore Gelyazka Amen."

The three of us left the apartment in silence and a little dazed. Our short hurried prayers seemed so inadequate. Surely Cancer needs more prayer than that. However, her next visit to the Hospital was to prove us wrong; the test results were inexplicably negative! The following Sunday Gelyazka was in Church testifying to what the Lord had done.

Her story reminds me of our first Cancer 'patient' in Troyan. Again the Lord had arranged it so that Andrew was with us. Before our visit one of the Church members had requested that we visit her when next in Troyan. She was undergoing chemotherapy and radiotherapy treatment, but her latest examination at the Hospital had shown she was still not clear.

I remember Katya, Andrew and myself strolling in the sunshine across the town square to her small house. We prayed aloud as we walked. This was often through desperation rather than spiritual 'maturity'. Many times our programme for the day was brim-full. We were painfully aware of how little time we were spending in prayer preparation. We relied heavily on God's Grace and favour, and on others – family and friends – who had been praying beforehand.

On this occasion I was far from full of faith.

"Lord, I don't do cancers!" I remember saying in protest! "I'm OK with smaller problems, but I've got no faith for this. Help us!" Fortunately I was with two friends who had!

I was not looking forward to the visit, or the repercussions if nothing happened. Even after dozens of miracles I was lacking faith for this one.

Katya knocked on the door. Immediately we were warmly invited in with much excitement and smiles. Jesus had got there ahead of us! That morning the latest test results found her completely clear. Her cancer had gone! The Hospital was baffled. So instead of praying, we thanked the Lord and sat down to a table full of food, prepared in celebration. "The doctors cannot understand it," she told us, " because the cancer had not been destroyed by the radiotherapy."

AN ELDERLY SAINT

One of my many hospitality visits was to the home of Persida. She was the sister of the Church Elder who had died under interrogation. Now in her 80's, Persida had seen it all come and go: life in pre-war Bulgaria; the annexation of the Balkans by the Nazis; the Communist 'liberation' and subsequent subjugation; the fall of the Iron Curtain in Eastern Europe; the collapse of Communism in Russia; the rise of corrupt government controlled by mafia power; and the ultimate dream of Bulgaria joining the E.E.C.

Persida had witnessed her Church go from freedom to persecution and back to freedom again. She reminisced with me about how the local government unsuccessfully attempted to close her Church down. She related stories of the contact with the West, and the 'Brother Andrew' couriers who travelled all the way from England by car with precious cargoes of Bibles. Persida and her husband had received these brave believers, given them hospitality, and used her basement as a storage depot for Bibles in transit to Romania. She reminded me of how dangerous such activity was in the 1970's (as it still is in the Communist and Muslim world today).

I loved to sit at the kitchen table with this elderly saint and listen and ask questions. In 1987 I had myself driven to Poland with two other Christians with a huge consignment of Bibles hidden in our vehicle. Now I was listening to the other side of the story. It humbled me, and reminded me how much we in the free West have, in terms of time, finance and opportunity (especially in our globe-trotting 21st. Century) – but also how easily we can squander the opportunities to serve those dependent on us for their very lives.

VILENA AND VILLE

Vilena was the only lady on the Church Council. An educated woman whose original ambition to be a doctor was abandoned when her father died. She married and had two children. But then tragedy struck again and her husband died. Her son had left full-time education; but her daughter, Ville, had stayed into the sixth form – the same school year as Bojana's grandson, Ivan.

Ville was an exceptional student with potential for enormous academic success; but without the financial means to achieve it. Even so she was applying to Sophia University, the 'Oxford' of Bulgaria, to study Telecommunications. It was important for the pride and prestige of the High School that applicants achieved the highest academic placements possible irrespective of whether they would ever be able to pursue such courses.

I learned all about Ville and her family from my first invitation to their home. On a subsequent visit to Troyan I was again invited. This time there were friends and family from Sophia. After the meal we all remained seated at the table and prayed. It was at this moment that something extraordinary happened. The Holy Spirit moved my heart very deeply. I stood up and spoke in front of all to Vilena's student daughter: "What your father on earth desired for you, your Father in Heaven will provide. You will go to Sophia University."

The words moved my heart and emotions so much that I burst into tears. I was utterly embarrassed; but no one else was. Instead a quiet peace descended on the gathering as we digested the words just spoken. At the heart of this family was a Father who cared and provided.

The Lord fulfilled His Word. Ville was offered a place at Sophia University, and achieved her Degree with the highest Honours and Distinction. She went on to complete her Masters with equal Distinction.

My second Troyan visit confirmed in my heart that the Lord was at the centre of what was going on, even if, at times, it didn't make a lot of sense to me. I had to stop trying to work out what it was all for; where it was going; what it was achieving. I *still* have no answer to these questions. Nevertheless, I was determined that while there was work for me to do I would go.

As well as removing any lingering doubts, my second visit proved to the Church in Troyan my commitment and sincerity. I was not a 'five day wonder', full of promises and intentions, destined never to return. Instead, the Church realized my commitment was deeper and longer term. They could rely on my return; and through Katya they could – and did – make appointments in anticipation of it happening.

Chapter Five

THE GYPSIES

Before Bulgaria I had little experience of Gypsies. I had never seen a Christian Gypsy in any Church, nor had I ever met one. I had not heard one preach, nor even heard the mention of Christian Gypsies in Church. As far as I, and the great majority of Christians in England were concerned, they simply didn't exist. This was to my shame when I discovered that the greatest Christian revival in the latter part of the Twentieth Century in England was among the Gypsies. 40% of the Gypsy population were now Born Again – 40%! How many Gypsy Churches did BBC TV's "Songs of Praise" ever visit? And how many Gypsy Church leaders were ever invited to share in mainstream Churches?

Gypsies make up about one tenth of the population of Bulgaria. They do not live on the edge of society as in England, but in the centre of the towns and villages in family communities. Their origins are essentially two-fold: Orthodox Christian Gypsies from the Balkans, and Islamic Gypsies from Turkey. For most the religious affiliation is cultural only. Even among the committed, few have either churches or mosques that they can call their own.

Before the Third Reich annexed the Balkans the Gypsies were free to enjoy their ancient nomadic way of life. But with Fascism came persecution and many tens of thousands were transported to Concentration Camps and murdered by the Nazis. The Soviet-controlled post-war government, eager to distance itself from its Racist foe, sought to protect them. But this was at a price. No longer would they be allowed the freedom to roam around. Instead they would cease to be nomadic and be settled in small communities within the towns and cities. In this way they would, as with the rest of the population, come under Soviet control.

These, then, are the Bulgarian Gypsies. To be Bulgarian (whether of Slav or of Greek origin) is to be a 'first class' member of society; to be Turkish is to be 'second class'; but to be gypsy renders you 'fifth class' – in fact you have no class at all!

Nor are the Bulgarians entirely unjustified in wishing to be kept at arms length from the Gypsies. Bulgarian Gypsy life can be unstable and violent, as well as loving and supporting. Among the non-Christians, the men gamble and drink most of the money they are able to make dealing in scrap. To survive, the local councils provide menial jobs such as road sweeping for the women so that they have the most basic of necessities for their families. In the worst cases, even this meagre amount is stolen, and families survive by begging and borrowing from each other.

When drunk the men can turn violent and often abuse their women. (Of course this happens in the Bulgarian and Turkish households also). But the Gypsy women have their own trump card up their sleeves—Witchcraft! When unjustly wronged or violated, the women seek amulets for protection and black magic spells (curses) for revenge. Voodoo-type dolls are sometimes used; black chickens are sacrificed. This dark and deadly evil often produces deep physical and psychological damage.

The use of such evils is not confined to the Gypsies alone. In many cases it is the Bulgarians and Turkish who are willing to seek out and pay for such practices. In Troyan it appeared to be a profitable cottage industry!

Yet among these small Gypsy communities I would meet strong and mature believers; and enjoy much blessing and fellowship among them.

Gypsies often attended meetings at Katya's Church, even if they were not always given the welcome they deserved. I was used to greeting these 'brown-faced' believers after the Services. But it was not until my third visit to Troyan that I was invited to one of their homes.

MILENA

Milena gave me my first invitation into a Gypsy home and my first taste of Gypsy hospitality. She had had a troubled life. Born into a Muslim Gypsy family, Milena had converted to Christianity in her late teens.

We in England have little experience of the yoke of Islam. It is a pernicious and devilish religion; totalitarian in outlook, and utterly ruthless in its control. For Christian converts, especially the women, vengeance is swift. There are only two penalties that Islam allows: expulsion or death. Because of the great shame that is brought on the family, only the removal of the source of such shame will bring back family honour. A stricter family will require murder to save the family honour; a more compassionate family will simply throw the 'infidel' out! If she has children, she loses them, together with all rights as parent and family member. In effect, she no longer exists, and the family will have no further contact with her.

Milena had been thrown out and disowned as a teenager. But her conversion was very strong, and the persecution from her family and friends only strengthened her faith and determination that others should know about Jesus. She had devoted much of her life to spreading the Gospel, encouraging home cell groups among the Gypsies – both in Bulgaria and around the Balkans. She had been a mighty warrior, and I could not but admire her devotion to Jesus.

Now she lived with her eight-year-old granddaughter. What had brought about this arrangement I didn't know, but they were totally devoted to each other. In Troyan, the little girl would be at all the meetings her grandma went to. In this way the little girl's love for Jesus was nourished with a remarkable depth of knowledge and understanding.

Milena's home was in another ancient row of buildings near the town centre. The house was a derelict wooden structure, with rambling wooden stairs open to the elements. Ceilings were falling down, and plaster crumbling. It was a risky business even getting into some of these homes. Stairs in particular were a hit and miss affair at the first climb. Milena only had money for the rent of two rooms, and was constantly behind with the payments! Even with such deprivation she always found a way to provide a two-litre bottle of Coca Cola and a packet of chocolate biscuits. Hospitality made in Heaven!

It became routine on my visits for Milena's granddaughter and I to visit the supermarket nearby and buy some groceries for her Nan. Somehow she always finished with the few coppers change in her pocket! I knew even this tiny gesture might create ill-feeling among other equally deprived families, but, for all her faults, Milena was quite alone, having paid a great price. I wanted to bless her.

In her tiny living room stood a small wooden stove, a bed, a sofa and some chairs. Milena had but a few splinters of wood for the fire. It seemed such a meagre and lonely existence for her, but then, before I had tasted my first biscuit, friends began to arrive. I soon learned the expect *anything* to happen at Milena's. Every visit was full of surprises. Gypsies of all ages turned up, from the youngest of children. No one seemed to have explained that ten year olds should be at ten year olds meetings; and fourteen year olds should go to teenage meetings!! *Everyone* came to Milena's meetings, and it was wonderful! Previously she had tried single-handedly to start and lead a Gypsy Church. It had ended in failure. But in her home the blessings flowed.

Here things happened that I could only dream about in England – ten year olds praying for adults; eighteen year olds laying hands on fourteen year olds to receive the Holy Spirit; eight year olds prophesying; teenagers being envisioned for ministry; everyone being caught up in the Spirit and singing in tongues; and when the Word of God came out – a room hungry to be taught. The fellowship was so natural and beautiful and spontaneous. So exciting were the visits that it was always hard to pull myself away for other appointments on my list.

Nor were Milena's meetings unique. In other Christian Gypsy homes I found the same love for Jesus in all ages, together with a unity in the Spirit when we prayed. Children of all ages appearing as if out of the woodwork! Toddlers wandering around bereft of nappies and sucking filthy dummies. Crying babies, being comforted by mother, sister, friend, neighbour? One never really knew. Young men waiting for something to do. Old men, sitting quietly in the corner, having long since learned not to interfere! Here were situations where the adage "Uncle Tom Cobley and all" rightly applied. How we need the Gypsies to teach us 'fellowship'. Truly, "where sin abounds, grace abounds even more" (Romans 5:12).

Yet into what seemed utter chaos, the Holy Spirit would find space to move among us. Jesus would heal headaches and toothaches and more serious ailments. Words of encouragement would be spoken. Singing and dancing would spontaneously happen. I had to learn the art, which they had perfected, of being unaware of the chaos around me. No one else noticed it, so neither should I.

A GYPSY FEAST

My first experiences of Gypsy hospitality had been full of blessing, and I wanted to meet more and know more. But the Gypsies are shy, and their communities rather closed to outsiders. Even the Christians in Troyan rarely stepped into Gypsy homes. I was motivated by my commission to "go to the Church in Troyan..." God has no concept of the Church as a building, or even denomination. The Believers *are* the Church, irrespective of where or how they meet. Even the leaderless Christian Gypsies were part of God's Church in Troyan. As such I wanted to hold out a hand of friendship.

An idea came into my imagination. I would sponsor a Gypsy Feast. I had no idea what this might mean in practice. Being the 'ignorant' Englishman, I could make the most ridiculous suggestions and be tolerated! I would pay for a sheep to be roasted and the gypsies would handle all the practical side.

I suggested the idea to Katya, and for the first time in nearly two years sensed a little unease. Her hesitation was justifiable. After all, I had never had my washing stolen, or my winter woodpile pilfered, or parts of my car gone missing. Katya knew full well that much of the meat from the sheep would 'disappear' long before the feast. And then there were the urgent repairs needed to the Church building. Wouldn't $100 do so much more in other ways?

Katya never voiced these concerns, but she was absolutely right. Money wasted on a sheep-roast seemed like money foolishly spent. It sounded like a foolish idea. But I felt it was also God's idea; and doesn't the New Testament say some positive things about the foolishness of God? Paul tells us that "the foolishness of God is wiser than man's wisdom"(1 Cor.1: 25). Let them steal all the meat! I was burdened to bless them, rather than feed them.

While still pondering these issues, a strange thing happened. Katya and I had been walking across derelict land near the back of some gypsy housing, when I noticed in a corner of the field a mound of soil about a metre in height. Katya was equally puzzled as to what it was, so we called over to a nearby Gypsy.

"Oh, that's the 'oven' where we cook the sheep when we have a Wedding Feast." he told us.

After that we both knew God was somehow in the idea, whatever it would bring.

"This is where I want us to have the Gypsy Feast", I said. "Let's get it in the diary for my next visit."

And we did. The Gypsy Feast was arranged to take place on the Saturday afternoon of my next visit, and at the place we had chosen. Everyone from the Gypsy community was invited, whether Orthodox or Evangelical or Muslim or Pagan. No one was excluded. And the Gypsies came, whether to get whatever was going or just out of curiosity.

Katya was a faithful steward of all the money, releasing it little by little for the gypsies to buy the food. Andrew came on this visit, and I was eager for him to sample Gypsy hospitality and Christian Fellowship Gypsy-style! We walked with Katya the few hundred metres to the feasting ground. There a long table had been prepared with paper tablecloths, cups and plates. I eagerly started to chat with as many people as possible, completely ignoring the food. Being a 'respectable Englishman' it was important that I didn't give the impression of only arriving for the food! Unfortunately I knew little about Gypsy culture. For them it *was* important I was there for the food! I was the Chief Guest, and as such, no one could eat until I had eaten and approved the Feast. My English manners were holding up proceedings!

"Look at this wonderful food" interrupted one of the Gypsy women. "You must come and taste it now".

I obliged.

At the very moment I tasted my first mouthful, something unbelievable happened. The heavens opened. A dark cloud that had unobtrusively parked itself directly over our gathering suddenly opened wide its celestial sluice gate! It rained violently. I had travelled the tropics, but I had never before experienced such violent rain. Within a minute everyone had scattered in panic. I looked around for shelter and noticed an articulated trailer standing about 70 metres away. My survival instinct drove me towards it as fast as I could run. Without a hesitation I dived under its rusting carcase.

The storm raged on for about ten minutes, and then it stopped as quickly as it had started. In ten minutes it had completely wiped out all the Gypsies' hard work. My precious feast had been washed away! I felt defeated, humiliated and confused. Had not God been at the centre of this? I wanted to cry out: "Lord, what are you doing?" but I didn't. Had not Katya been right all along in showing little enthusiasm for it? Was it not simply my own silly stunt?

I crawled out from under the trailer. Everything and everyone had disappeared. No Andrew. No Katya. No Feast! Only an empty rain-soaked wooden table remained, as if to mock me: 'Look! No feast!'

I assumed Katya and Andrew must have made their way back to her home. But instead of following them, for some unknown reason I went instead into one of the small tenement blocks that housed the Gypsies. I found myself in a building I had never been in before. As I walked up the steps I could hear voices. I followed the noise, and could hear singing.

I opened the door. Inside was an assembly of about fifty Gypsies, some of whom I recognised, having a Praise Party. There was spontaneous singing and testimonies, Bible readings and dancing, Gypsy Christian music coming from clapped out instruments, and young children praying in the

Spirit. I was enthralled; and being eager not to disturb the meeting I sneaked to the back. I watched in amazement. What a sight! Satan had destroyed our lamb roast, but God had provided a better Feast!

After 20 minutes Andrew came through the door, followed after a few minutes by Katya. We experienced that day how occasionally the Holy Spirit pours Himself out like a monsoon, a great flood, on his people. Something new was happening among the Christian Gypsies. God was bringing them together. God was envisioning them to meet together. Within twelve months there would be a new Gypsy Church in Troyan.

From that day on I loved the Gypsies. God gave me a special heart of compassion for them. I refused to listen to any word of criticism of them, knowing only too well what rogues many of them were. And from that day doors opened for me in every corner of the Gypsy community.

JIFCA

Jifca lived with a Turkish Gypsy extended family of around twenty people. Their home was a mixture of buildings. A house that appeared unfinished, together with an assortment of large wooden shacks in the garden. For our first visit we were invited into the house. Once they began to trust us we shared fellowship in the shack.

Their invitation had no specific purpose other than to offer hospitality tinged with curiosity. We sat down and I was surrounded by about fifteen women and children, with two men in the shadows. I thanked them for their invitation and each one began to introduce themselves. At the end of the introductions I noticed that one of the women had not spoken.

"What about you?" I asked. "What is your name?"

One of her friends quickly spoke for her: "This is Jifca. She was born deaf. She cannot hear anything."

Jifca was twenty-six years old, with a common law marriage but no children. In every way she was the 'Cinderella' of this extended family. Compassion filled my heart. I had learned in the two years of visiting Troyan that it was not my place to look for people and problems to pray for. The Lord would bring them to me. I only had to respond to *their* requests. This was also the New Testament pattern. Jesus never went up to the sick and asked if they would like to be healed. Rather, needy people inundated Him. They cried out from a distance. They begged His intervention. They fell at His feet in desperation. Many times He was overwhelmed and had to escape the crowds by travelling deep into the wilderness to be alone with His Father. In Church meetings we invariably follow this New Testament pattern. We may often ask for people with needs to "come to the front" for prayer; but we never walk around the meeting targeting them personally.

But on this day, that is exactly what I did. Where had my wisdom gone? Had I not learnt that it is God who brings the requests for prayer to me? Unfortunately my compassion for Jifca overruled. I asked if we could pray for her. Immediately expectations in the room were raised. Immediately I realised my mistake! What had I done?

We asked more questions about her deafness. Because she could not hear, she could not speak. She knew signing, and was able to lip-read. She had 10% hearing in one ear and a little more in the other. In practice she heard nothing except extremely loud noises directly into her ear, and even this only translated as an unintelligible faint sound. She communicated by signing and a few grunts, which were intelligible only to her family. We prayed. Nothing seemed to happen, but I promised to visit her again. .

Six months went by. There seemed to be little change. But Jifca was on the top of my list when I next visited with Andrew. We all prayed again. As we prayed the Lord spoke to me: "Go and buy a Personal Hifi from town". These small cassette machines with headphones were available at the electrical shop. The instruction came so loud and clear into my mind. Of course!! Why hadn't *I* thought of that? I quickly excused myself, jumped into my Hire Car, and went shopping.

By now I was not only familiar with the town of Troyan, but also how to make my way to the Christian Bookshop in the heart of the capital Sofia. I had been introduced to this wonderful resource by one of Ville's friends who lived in Sofia. Once I could locate it, it became my first stopping off point when visiting Bulgaria. I made a point of stocking up with Christian tracts, leaflets and music – both Bulgarian and Gypsy.

The Bible urges us to "always be prepared to give an answer to everyone who asks you to give the reason for the hope that you have" (1 Peter 3:15). So it was important for me to have available in the car tracts that explained in the Bulgarian language *how* to become a Christian. Had I not been given one by the Rev. Keenan when I first invited Jesus into my heart? And did not this little booklet, with its simple pictures and explanations, speak more to my heart than all of my six years of theological study?

So I was excited. When God speaks I get excited. I had the cassette, the batteries, and a special gift of two tapes of Gypsy Christian music. I returned within 15 minutes, much to everyone's bewilderment. We prayed that this new resource would bless Jifca, that she would be able to hear and understand the Gypsy words and music. She pressed the 'play' button and as I turned the volume up her face beamed with delight. Not only could she hear it, but, even more remarkably, she understood the words, *even though she had never heard anyone speaking before*. We left her totally absorbed in what she was listening to.

The following morning Jifca was in Church, still listening to the tapes! Although unable to hear what was going on in the service, she followed every word of the hymns and songs. Jifca was obviously highly intelligent. Although dumb and deaf, Jifca had learnt to read and write. After the Service she copied down the words of the hymns we had sung onto a scrap of paper. Through the music tapes Jifca had heard of a Saviour who loved her and gave His life for her. She had heard Jesus speaking through the Gypsy songs and responded. From that day she came to Katya's Church twice every Sunday.

Her conversion had a profound impact on her extended family. There were only one or two Christians, the rest were Turkish Muslim gypsies. Later at least four converted to Christianity and joined the Gypsy Church.

With the help of my friends in Sofia, Andrew and I arranged for Jifca to have a proper hearing assessment at a private clinic. The diagnosis was encouraging. By now she had 40% hearing in her good ear, enough for a hearing aid. The fittings were ordered and a special visit was made bringing Jifca all the way to the Capital to have her hearing aid fitted. I will never forget the indescribable joy on her face at *hearing her own voice* for the very first time.

God had miraculously broken into her hopeless silent world. She had found Jesus, and through miracle and medicine she had new ears.

ENKA'S SQUINT

Another Gypsy family lived two hundred metres along the street from Katya's family. Their house was built on a small piece of waste ground just beyond where the homes of the Bulgarians terminated. Another wooden shack with earthen floors – but it was still custom to remove shoes at the door!

This family were different. Grandma and grandad were Christians, and that patriarchal love for Jesus had a profound influence over the entire family. The place was recognised by the Gypsies as a Christian home, and many Sunday meetings took place here prior to the Gypsy Church being started.

I had been invited to meet everyone, and everyone turned out to meet me: the toddlers, the baby, the six year olds with their friends; older and older children; young teenage mothers; the boys, fighting with the girls for a ringside seat; and in the background, grandma and granddad. The place was packed, and they were ready for action!

A small table stood in the tiny space still unoccupied at the centre of the room, proudly displaying Coca-Cola and chocolate biscuits. Even the smallest children knew that *no one* was allowed the biscuits except Pastor Allan! But it didn't stop them focussing their eyes and imagination on what they might taste like. The little ones had one eye on me and one eye on the biscuits. So when I was invited to help myself, the children went unusually quiet.

In Asian custom all the food technically belongs to the honoured guest, and he can eat as much as he desires. It is his prerogative whether he eats the entire packet of biscuits or shares them out.

"Would it be alright if the children had a biscuit as well?" I asked.

Within seconds the locusts had politely but efficiently emptied the packet!

The family were well used to home meetings, with testimonies, shared Scriptures, praise, prayer, prophecy and healings. As always the Holy Spirit came among us as we worshipped. Gypsy music is very similar to Jewish music and makes praise dancing so easy. The children loved it and beamed when they saw I was joining in too. Finally we all sat down.

Someone asked if there were any prayer needs. One of the children had toothache. We prayed. I encouraged some of the children to join me in laying hands on his head and shoulders.

"How are you feeling?" I asked him when we had finished.

"It's gone!" he replied.

As we prayed for others I couldn't help noticing a young girl of around eleven years old. Enka had a terrible squint in her left eye, which turned the iris completely out of sight into her head. Such a disability brought with it many problems. Apart from the obvious difficulty of her sight, she suffered from low self-esteem from a lifetime of taunts and insults. And then there were her marriage prospects. Young pretty Gypsy girls in Bulgaria married at fifteen or sixteen. Often they were fought over by the men. But Enka's chances of finding a husband would be slim; and, as with Jifca, my compassion took over. I broke the golden rule again

"I would like to pray for you," I said gently. "Is that OK?"

"Da" she replied.

We prayed, and nothing happened. But being a stubborn Yorkshire man, I was not prepared to leave it there. I waited until later when Katya and I met in her kitchen to discuss the day's happenings.

"I'm determined that Enka's eye is healed." I said. " And so I want to pay for the operation myself. But for this to happen Enka needs someone in the family to take her to the Hospital and attend all the appointments. Can you talk to Enka's Grandma and see if she will agree to this?"

Katya obliged. Enka's Grandma assured us she would take her granddaughter to all the appointments. It was through the faith, prayers and sheer determination of this Christian family that Enka was healed.

The Hospital in Troyan did not undertake eye operations. Enka had to travel the thirty miles south to Plovdiv. Gypsies are not so welcome in most of Bulgaria's hospitals. First, they have no money, so no one is interested in their problems. Secondly they are notoriously unreliable, finding the discipline of keeping appointments difficult. Thirdly, they have no means to pay for the travel to other towns for specialist treatment. And finally, they are seen as dirty and sources of unwanted infections in the Hospital.

While I was back in England, Katya meticulously organized the finance for Enka's journeys to Plovdiv. "Tell the doctor the Englishman will pay for everything", I had encouraged her. It had little effect. Nine months of regular visits resulted in little help, save for some correction spectacles to wear! They were being fobbed off, but Enka's grandma persisted. Soon after they were given another doctor, and Enka's name was immediately put to the top of his surgery list!

Finally, Enka was given the date for her admission. In my excitement I promised to travel to Plovdiv from England to visit her in Hospital: after all, I had a bill to pay. She was due for admission on the Friday, with the operation on the Saturday, and confinement in Hospital until the following Wednesday. That weekend I travelled to Troyan especially to keep my promise. I visited the family at their home and heard everything was going well.

On the Monday morning I drove to the Plovdiv Hospital to visit her, as I had promised, and also to pay the bill. Having parked the car, I walked the short distance to the Main Entrance, only to see Enka and her Grandma standing at the door! Enka had been discharged two days early. She carefully took the cotton wool pad from her eye to reveal a beautiful lovely straight eye – with virtually no redness or bruising. I couldn't believe what I was looking at.

"But what about the bill?" I asked. "Where's the bill?"

"No bill." replied Grandma. "No bill." She repeated, laughing.

The three of us walked to the car. "I don't believe it." I kept saying to myself. "No bill? That's impossible. This is Bulgaria. It just never happens."

As we travelled in the car back to Troyan we were all quiet and reflective. What had happened was amazing. Was this not the most wonderful thing that God had done? And now we were going home to show the world. Enka's family knew we were on our way. They lived on the other side of the river from Grandma. Enka's parents were not Christians, and had given little encouragement to their daughter.

Everyone was standing around waiting for her; her parents, her four younger brothers and sisters, her friends, the neighbours, other grandparents, younger and older gypsies curious to see the outcome. We got out of the car. Everyone was in tears. *Everyone!* No one could believe it. A young girl's life changed *forever*! Old and young men alike were crying. Enka's younger brothers were in tears. Her successful surgery seemed to have touched the hearts of the entire Gypsy population.

It also softened the men's hearts. Before that day it was rare for the gypsy men to share in the fellowship when I visited. They were always around, and always friendly; but they were just uninterested. After Enka's operation their attitude changed; there were men in the middle wherever I went among the Gypsies. They had seen something they believed could not happen. Enka would forever be a living reminder of God's grace and compassion.

The following day Katya and I were invited for the first time into Enka's parents' home. It was a wooden, one-roomed hovel built halfway up a muddy hillside. How her parents and five children lived like that I cannot guess. But their gratitude far outweighed any embarrassment they might have felt at inviting a 'rich' Englishman to their meagre dwelling. Coca-Cola and biscuits were again on offer, but Enka's mother was quiet and shy.

Before we arrived Katya explained a little of the family history. Enka's mother, although having five children including an eleven year old, was still only 26 years old. She had Enka at the age of fifteen, an unusually young age even for the Gypsies. Enka's mother had been given the opportunity to have her daughter's eye corrected when Enka was still a toddler, but she had not taken up the offer. As this free provision was only for very young children, she later lost the opportunity. She must have bitterly regretted that. Afterwards it was impossible to find the money to pay for the treatment.

The whole family was present that day when I visited, and we all together gave thanks to the Lord for the wonderful thing that had happened. There was little else to say, and I was about to leave when the Holy Spirit stirred in my heart and gave me some words of blessing to share privately with Enka's mother. She was sitting between Katya and myself, so it was easy to speak quietly and for Katya to whisper the translation into her ear:

"My dear child, I know all about you. I have loved you since the foundation of the world. I have never stopped loving you; and I want you to know that you are accepted and forgiven. Receive my forgiveness into your heart, and I will take away all your guilt and shame and crown your life with good things."

The words poured out of my heart, but they were for her and her alone. Amazingly, with everyone squashed into this tiny home, no one appeared to hear or take any notice. It was as if the angels had covered their eyes and ears.

God's Word spoke very deeply into her soul. When we had finished she gave us the most beautiful smile. It was the first time I ever saw her smile. From that moment her countenance changed. She had heard Jesus speaking into her life. It changed her completely. After that she began to go to Gypsy Christian meetings.

A PROBLEM OF ANGER

For the most part the Christian Gypsies ministered to each other. I did not have queues of them coming for my help. They knew the principles of how to pray, and they got on with it. But there were exceptions, and one was a Christian Gypsy lady who I had come to know and respect for her spiritual maturity.

"I need your help, Pastor Allan, but I don't want to talk about it here."

Katya and I arranged to meet her in the Church building where it would be quiet and private. We used this building on many occasions when home situations made confidentiality impossible.

She wasted no time in relating her story. In the previous four months she had suddenly and inexplicably developed an uncontrollable anger problem. The anger would rise up in her without warning, and be violently out of control. Before this started four months earlier she had never in her life had a problem with anger. Her behaviour was reaping havoc with her family, especially with her teenage children, and afterwards she would feel deep guilt and shame at how she had behaved. Even after many friends' prayers there was no change. She was desperate.

One important lesson I had learned in Troyan was the difference between the problem and the *symptom*. So many times Christians make the mistake of praying for the symptom rather than the problem. Until the problem is exposed and dealt with God is very reluctant to remove the symptoms.

An obvious example of these symptoms is physical pain. It is like a fire alarm, which demands our attention and alerts us when something is wrong. Simply praying for the symptoms is often as effective as asking the Fire Brigade to put out the blaze by turning their hoses on the alarms! Once the real problem of the fire is found, the alarms are switched off. In the same way, once we find and deal with the real problem, the symptom – whether pain or something else—goes away. This is perhaps the single most important reason why prayers for healing appear to go unanswered—*we are praying for the symptoms only*!

Differentiating between symptom and problem is not always easy. In Troyan I often illustrated this problem with reference to the Doctor's Surgery:

Imagine a footballer breaking his arm and going off to the Doctor.

"What's the problem?" the Doctor asks.

"I've got a terrible pain in my arm" the footballer replies.

"Oh, I can soon cure that." The doctor responds, and hands over a prescription for Paracetamol!

The footballer presented the symptom (pain) and not the problem (a broken bone). The doctor doesn't ask any questions, and assumes the pain is the problem. Unfortunately our praying can also be at this level: no questions asked, and 'problems' accepted as presented.

There may be reasons for this. The one being prayed for may not want any personal questions asked – 'let's leave it in the past!'; 'let bygones be bygones'; 'let's not rake up the past'; 'what's dead is gone!'; 'let's not bring anybody else into it'. The intercessor may be too embarrassed to ask difficult and perhaps challenging questions. He or she may also be reluctant to disturb painful memories, which risk stirring up even more pain or guilt. In these and other ways the problems are left buried and only the symptoms are available for prayer.

For severe pain in the arm, a doctor's proper course of action is two-fold: first, ask questions and make a preliminary examination to identify the problem; and second, use the X-ray machine for a more detailed examination. *Before praying for healing we always need a proper course of action.*

I had listened carefully to the Gypsy lady, and my first question was to clarify the nature of this anger. Was this natural or supernatural? Was its source the human spirit or an evil spirit? If the anger is natural and from the human spirit, then it is within that person's control. Anger in itself is not a sin; it is uncontrollable anger that grieves the Holy Spirit.

" 'In your anger do not sin': Do not let the sun go down while you are still angry, and do not give the devil a foothold." (Ephesians 4:26,27)

When the anger is outside our control, *who* is controlling it? Paul in this quote from Ephesians makes it clear: if we lose control of our anger we risk allowing the devil to bring in his own system of control; that is, demonic control.

When asked, the Gypsy lady readily admitted that when the anger rose up in her she lost all control. When it subsided again, she was grieved and shocked at her own behaviour. I shared that it appeared to be a spirit of anger – an enemy from outside – and she readily agreed.

When praying for healing, I never start praying out the problem until I have that assurance of peace from the Holy Spirit that the problem has been fully exposed. The spirit of anger was only the *symptom*, and as such, *it would have been futile to pray for deliverance at this point.* To find the *problem* I now had to search, like an X-ray machine, into the pain. Why had this spirit come into such a mature Christian's life?

This little word "why?" is such an important tool when we pray for others. Never assume you have all the information until you no longer need to ask the question "why?"

I asked if something unusual had happened four months earlier when the anger began.

"Da...... Da......" She started. "My father died suddenly, and I had no time to talk to him before he died. All my life I had a wonderful relationship with my father. We were so very close and never had any disagreement. We loved each other deeply. But about two years ago we had a very strong and hurtful argument and we didn't speak after that. I had resolved to forgive my father and ask his forgiveness, but before I could do this ... he just died! I became so very angry with him for dying without speaking to me, and without being forgiven."

Her testimony was uncompromisingly open and honest.

We all prayed together: "Lord help us. Teach us how to pray."

After a few minutes I suggested something to her.

"I want you to imagine your father sitting in that empty chair in front of you. And I want you to share your feelings of anger and guilt and sin and forgiveness that you were preparing to share with him. This is not talking to the dead, but asking the Holy Spirit to help you *imagine* him still alive. In effect the Holy Spirit is helping you to go back and complete what you were cut off from doing ... confessing your sin to him and forgiving his sin against you."

She understood exactly what I was asking. While she talked, and cried, and confessed her sin, Katya and I prayed aloud in tongues. When she finished Katya ministered to her: "The Lord heal and forgive and restore you."

Of course there was still the spirit of anger. The Gypsies had prayed with her about this, and rightly recognized the demonic nature of the anger. They were quite capable of ministering deliverance; but this had been the symptom rather than the problem. That's why their prayers had been unsuccessful.

With everything confessed and repented of, there were no chains holding down this Spirit of Anger. We bound it, and commanded it out.

We prayed for the Holy Spirit to renew and refill her heart, to restore her love for her family and heal all the hurts caused by the anger.

It never returned.

Chapter Six

FOUR INSTITUTIONS OF TROYAN

THE ORPHANAGE

All Bulgarian towns have an orphanage and Troyan was no exception. When I learned of its existence I wanted to visit. I had no mandate from the Lord, and there was nothing practical I could offer. But I had to visit.

After all the stories that surfaced in the 1990's concerning Romanian orphans, I was expecting the worst. To my surprise the large Victorian building, built in the Nineteenth Century by Christian missionaries, was clean and in good repair. The Director met me with warmth and interest, even though I explained I had no big dollar organization behind me. The staff were friendly and eager to show me around, but they were also very demoralised. The government gave little support and they had not been paid in months. Even so, their care of the children was exemplary.

Many of the children were not orphans at all. There were children of young mothers unable to cope. There were also many Gypsy children. The Gypsies, desperately poor and in overcrowded housing, occasionally decided it would be better for the child to be brought up in the Orphanage. Sometimes the parents of these children visited regularly. For other children, their parents had little interest. They would come for them when they were old enough to look after themselves!

The children ranged in age from two to ten years old. At that age they were transferred to the senior orphanage in Plovdiv. Katya and I visited this place too. As with the younger ones, the older children were healthy, clean and well clothed.

The little ones had toys and other things for play. Some of the younger staff were keen to provide reading, writing, and other creative lessons outside of school to stimulate the brighter ones. In the neglected garden was a well-worn children's playground with swings and slides etc. which the children loved.

I suppose in my heart I wanted someone from England to come and get involved with this, but it never happened. All I was able to do was to commit myself to a visit every time I came to Troyan, and that I did. For £50 I filled the car with sacks of potatoes, carrots and other vegetables, and some fresh fruit. Knowing the plight of the staff, I made a point of suggesting to the Director that the staff could enjoy some of these gifts. In that way they were able to take home food for their own families with a clear conscience.

THE HIGH SCHOOL

Another Institution I visited was one of the two High Schools in Troyan. This was the town's 'Grammar School' of learning, achieving many scholarships to Sofia University. Again I had no commission from the Lord to do anything, neither did I attempt to. But the friendship with the Headmistress did bring other rewards. A pupil exchange scheme was eventually started between the Troyan School and South Normanton High School in Derbyshire.

THE HOSPITAL

From the first, my instruction from the Lord had been unwavering and crystal clear: "Go to the Church in Troyan and pray for them; and also go to the Hospital." If I had been uncertain what the first part might involve, the second part was more straightforward. Through my wife's work as a General Practitioner, she had many contacts within and outside the N.H.S. I was sure there would be benefits for the Hospital in Troyan, whatever its circumstances.

Without knowing a Hospital existed in Troyan I took it upon myself on my very first visit to bring a suitcase full of medicines, both in date and out of date! Through my wife these were easy to come by. Annette simply begged the Reps (salesmen) of the Pharmaceutical Companies for help. Their assistance over four years was extremely appreciated. I made it a practice to bring a suitcase of medicines on every visit. I was also able to procure a redundant Health Service E.C.G. Heart Testing Machine. Everything was openly declared at the customs in Sofia Airport, and I never once had a problem. I was aware how feeble this small contribution was, but through these efforts valuable relationships were established.

The Health Service in Bulgaria was still organised according to the old Soviet centralised system. This was very different from what we enjoy. There were no General Practitioners and no Family Doctors. Almost all the medical assistance was contained within the Hospital. In this Institution the doctors were all specialists in specific areas of medicine.

Every sick person in Troyan had to make contact with the Hospital. Because of this the Hospital officials were aware of anyone mysteriously recovering. After a time even the Hospital Director was taking note!

On my very first day in Troyan, having found myself at the Hospital praying for Kalinka, I had made an appointment to see the Hospital Director, Dr. Bambov. Here was the man on whose shoulders the entire health of the town depended. A man of enormous skill and responsibility; and into his office I walked for the first time, carrying my suitcase like the Spiv (illegal trader) out of BBC TV's "Dad's Army"!

I nervously introduced myself, deliberately avoiding the word "God"! That would come later. Indeed Dr. Andrew later presented Dr. Bambov with his very own Gideon Bible, which he warmly received. But on my first appearance it would not have been helpful to announce "God sent me here"! Instead, I explained as much as I thought he would be able to accept at this first meeting. I had come to Troyan to visit the Church. My wife was a Family Doctor, and I wanted to help the Hospital in some small way. I then opened the suitcase, and, much to my embarrassment, half the medicines fell out onto the floor!

At that point I'm not sure who was the most embarrassed. It was obvious I was struggling. I'm sure Dr. Bambov was also waiting for the 'catch'! ("What does he *really* want?" he must have been thinking to himself.). Nobody brings piles of medicines for nothing. Even the Drug Companies have long-term strategies attached to their charitable aid. Dr. Bambov must have wondered what I was up to. Perhaps he thought I would ask to go round the wards to pray for people. But that was never my intention. My commission was never to "go to the hospital and pray for them", but to "go to the *Church* and pray for them." My place in the Hospital was no more than an offer of friendship and practical support. Once Dr. Bambov realised this, our mutual respect blossomed. Instead of asking for favours, I simply asked if there were any special types of medicines I could bring from England. He made a few suggestions, and I left a grateful if bewildered Dr. Bambov.

Every visit to Troyan brought the same routine to the Orphanage and Hospital. After the third time I could see that Dr. Bambov really was beginning to believe that no strings were attached. However, the most important help to him came not from myself but from Dr. Andrew. The day I turned up with Andrew Dr. Bambov beamed with delight. I had not been invited onto a single Ward, but Andrew was given a two-hour tour of the entire establishment!

Apart from the obvious dialogue and medical camaraderie that bonded these two doctors, there was one other important reason for Andrew's warm reception. The medicalworld of Bulgaria was about to be turned on its head. The Bulgarian Parliament had decided to change from the Soviet centralised system of medical care to the British Health Service system. The change had enormous repercussions. Surgeries, which didn't exist in Bulgaria, would have to suddenly come into being. Doctors, who had studied in specialist fields, would now have to quickly become all-round General Practitioners. Instead of working in the security of the Hospital system, they would now have to procure their own building, backup staff and systems. The great majority of doctors in Bulgaria had two years' notice to retrain as General Practitioners. What a task! And, of course, nobody had the slightest idea how to run a G.P. Surgery. Few had travelled outside the Eastern Bloc.

Dr. Bambov knew how precious was Andrew's experience in a 30-year career as a Family Doctor, and he was eager that his staff should learn from it. So Andrew was invited to be the guest speaker at a one-day conference for the local doctors, to be held in Troyan, and having the title: "The Work of a Family Doctor". The most basic of topics would be covered: the length of appointments; procedures for referrals; home visits; financing support staff; the design of buildings; holiday cover and many more. The questions were endless.

On the day of the conference, as Andrew was preparing to stand up and give his opening address, something amazing happened. Dr. Bambov interjected with an unplanned introduction.:

" Dr. Andrew and Pastor Allan are the two men from England whose prayers are responsible for many of the sudden and inexplicable recoveries from serious illness. I myself have personally witnessed some of these miraculous recoveries, where the only explanation I can offer is God's divine intervention."

This was totally unexpected, and took Andrew completely by surprise. He was still stunned by the words later that evening when he shared what had happened. We had both avoided 'plastering' Dr. Bambov with religion. In so doing we had given him the freedom to draw his own conclusions; and he had used this important occasion to publicly make his views known.

THE PRISON

If walking through the door of the Hospital and requesting a meeting with the Director was relatively easy, the same approach would hardly work with the town's prison! Fortunately it wasn't necessary. Katya's father, Pastor Peter, had been faithfully and diligently visiting the prisoners every fortnight for a long time. When I discovered this I was eager to accompany him.

Troyan has a large prison on the edge of town, with inmates of every category from petty thieves to rapists and murderers. For a poor East European country the standard of care was high. The Commandant was Colonel Marin Vachevski, an experienced army officer. He was a hunk of a man with a congenial smile and searching eyes that penetrated through the superficialities of life. He was a man of authority, and no fool; but he was also a man who cared. When the prisoners had rioted soon after his appointment he had incurred the wrath of his superiors by *not* going in with rubber bullets and teargas. Instead he listened to the grievances, promised change, and ended the standoff without violence. This one act singled him out as a remarkable Prison Governor, and his reputation and respect among the inmates was established.

He had also bent the rules for me. Visiting outside normal hours was a rare privilege, but the Director made a point of allowing all Christian Pastors access to the prisoners, irrespective of denomination. In a strictly Orthodox country, this was rare indeed. A more difficult obstacle to my visiting was the "no women" rule. Without Katya to translate it was impossible to speak to the prisoners. Again Colonel Marin made an exception for me.

On my first visit I immediately warmed to the man. He was extremely intelligent, quick-witted and very knowledgeable. Perhaps the sheer lack of intellectual stimulation in such a job warmed me to him. Perhaps he also enjoyed my gritty straight-talking Yorkshire character! He asked me questions on every subject except religion; and our conversations would linger for up to an hour at every visit. He was hungry to learn from my travels in India and Pakistan, the Far East and Vietnam; and he constantly asked me my opinions about the big issues facing the world – Communism, corruption, the E.E.C., China, immigration and the like. His own breadth of understanding was amazing. To add to the mix I treated him to a few doses of Yorkshire humour which he enjoyed and reciprocated. I often wondered if my reputation had gone before me – perhaps through the Hospital Director – because Colonel Marin seemed somehow to know what I was doing in Troyan without ever asking me.

We measured each other up and were pleased with what we found. From my first visit Colonel Marin gave me a personal invitation to visit the Prison whenever I was in Troyan. I willingly obliged.

This was the first time I had *ever* been inside a prison. And now I was going to speak to about thirty incarcerated Bulgarians. I felt quite inadequate. I kept hearing a little voice saying, "keep the message simple, keep the message simple." So I told them a story about a man who regularly went metal detecting, and one day found a hoard of old gold coins in a farmer's field. He knew he couldn't steal them because they couldn't be sold without legal documents. So he sold his home and possessions – everything he had – and offered the farmer double value for the field. The farmer was delighted to accept the deal. Now the gold was legally his (see Matthew 13:44). The message was simple: "If you really want Jesus in your life, it will cost you everything, but you will always gain more than you lose."

After my talk, someone seized the opportunity he had been waiting for:

" I am an innocent man and have been unjustly sentenced. Can you help me?"

I was not expecting this, and felt trapped. It was not my place to discuss their unjust sentences. I had a responsibility to Colonel Marin, whose authority I was under.

"Help, Lord," I prayed in my thoughts. "Give me Wisdom."

Words came into my mind and boldness into my spirit. I spoke very firmly to them all:

"Some of you are here unjustly because you are innocent. But some of you are murderers and are only serving a sentence for theft! Don't tell me this place is unjust. All life is unjust. It's what you *DO* about it that will make or break you." I then told them about how unjust Jesus' sentence was, a man innocent of all crime.

There was silence. No prisoner ever complained about his plight to me again.

Six months later I was in Troyan again. Colonel Marin's first question to me was this: "what do you think about the prisoners?" He was testing me. He never asked me anything about the Prison that he didn't already know. I told him exactly what happened. Not only that, but a copy of every tract and leaflet that I brought in for the prisoners I placed on his desk for his approval.

"If anything meets with your disapproval, I will omit it," I said. He never questioned anything.

A genuine friendship developed between this man and myself. We loved our conversations. We loved each other's frankness and honesty. Neither of us was afraid to share exactly what we were thinking. To show my appreciation and friendship, I wanted to bring a gift from England. I decided on a bottle of Single Malt Scotch Whisky! Some will say this was unwise. I probably made a mistake. But it seemed an appropriate gift for Colonel Marin. So at every subsequent visit, when we presented our Passports and ourselves at the Prison gate for inspection, I would be carrying a gift-wrapped parcel. It was never inspected or inquired about. It was the Governor's Whisky!

The ministry among the prisoners was Pastor Peter's. I was simply enjoying the fruit of his labour. My only small contribution was to bring dozens and dozens of Bulgarian Christian magazines and tracts for Christian prisoners. Of course many of them couldn't read! Of course many tried to sell them for a couple of cigarettes! But the Word of God got into the Prison, and perhaps also into some prison warders' homes.

Chapter Seven

THE RESTAURANT

Troyan is an ancient mountain town, but there is little of its old heritage left. The Communists cared little about preserving relics of a previous culture; they were too busy establishing their own Soviet-style culture. Those who retained legal ownership of these older properties during this time had neither the finance nor resources to maintain such buildings. As a result only a few dozen very old buildings were still standing, and most were in a dreadful state of disrepair.

The Restaurant, therefore, stood out as a rare exception. Near the centre of town, and the end building on a row of derelict timber-framed homes, this building demanded to be noticed. It alone had been carefully and professionally restored. Aside from all the pavement cafes and coffee bars, it was the only proper restaurant I ever found in Troyan. Some farsighted entrepreneur had obviously decided that one day Troyan would need a quality restaurant, and this would be it.

The place became my oasis. As there were so few customers, it was always quiet. Here I could escape and relax. At the end of a non-stop day, when Katya had to get back for the children's' bedtime, it was the perfect place to unwind. Here I could come with Andrew and other visitors and discuss our thoughts about the day just ended. We hardly ever came for food because we were never hungry!

The Restaurant also served as a place where I could offer back a little of the hospitality given to me. It was a tangible way of showing appreciation. My first 'guests' were, naturally, Katya's entire family! On another occasion I invited Dr. Bambov and his wife. They had very kindly welcomed Dr. Andrew and myself to their home for an evening meal, and the restaurant was my 'little piece of England' in which I could return the favour. This also seemed an ideal opportunity to include the new Church Pastor and his wife.

THE NEW PASTOR

News of a New Pastor at Katya's Church came as a complete surprise to me. Of course I knew the Church was desperate for a new leader, and that Pastor Peter was only 'holding the fort' until an appointment could be made. The opportunities were few, and they had jumped at the chance when a young man offered to come to Troyan.

The young Pastor was inexperienced, in contrast to Peter; but with elders of Peter's calibre, and a heart to learn from the experience of others, youth would be no disadvantage. Two days earlier I had visited the new Pastor's home and met his wife and young family. The Restaurant now provided the perfect venue for introductions. The new Pastor and his wife round the same table as the Hospital Director and his wife; together with Katya, Dr. Andrew and myself.

Unfortunately a clash of cultures threatened the harmony of the whole evening. The problem arose over the drinking of alcohol! Now it is important to understand that Bulgaria is one of those countries (e.g. Russia, and increasingly Great Britain) where alcohol is rarely used as a social drink, but mostly as a drug, by which to get inebriated as quickly as possible. So when Bulgarians sit down for a special meal there are three glasses by their placing; for beer, for wine and for spirits. And all three are drunk simultaneously! This is not the extreme, this is the cultural norm.

The cultural divide could not have been more contrasting. Here was the Pentecostal Pastor, a champion of teetotalism; and the overworked Orthodox doctor, enjoying his tipple to unwind after another stressful day. And in the middle? An English doctor and 'Pastor' who liked a drink occasionally with their meals!

The drinks waiter arrived. The Bambovs ordered the traditional Bulgarian three-course tipple! Katya and the Pastor ordered orange juice. Then all eyes turned on Andrew and myself. Katya knew we drank alcohol in England – we never pretended otherwise. We had also enjoyed a glass of wine at the Bambovs. Andrew spoke first and ordered a glass of wine, and I did the same. The atmosphere seemed to freeze over! I attempted to melt it with a joke about Paul's advice to Timothy to "use a little wine because of your stomach and your frequent illnesses" (1 Timothy 5:23). It was of little help. In the eyes of the new Pastor I was conforming to the world.

On reflection, all of us from England should have decided in advance to be teetotal in Bulgaria on all occasions, because this was the guidance of the Pentecostal Church leadership in Bulgaria. We should have followed their example. This had, for example, always been the pattern I had adopted when meeting with the Church in Vietnam – a country with similar alcoholism problems. Unfortunately we were unaware of the scale of alcoholism in Bulgaria. Having established a pattern, we were correct to stick to it – though Andrew and I only ever drank two glasses of wine in Troyan. And I *never* regretted my choice of gift to the Prison Governor.

Religious legalism quenches the Holy Spirit. It destroys what the Lord begins to build, and creates hypocrisy and hardheartedness. I had stepped on the golden Pentecostal rule in Bulgaria: "Pentecostals don't drink alcohol". The rest of the meal was polite and friendly, but the Spirit of God had not remained with us.

DONKA'S DEPARTING

Other occasions in the restaurant were much more joyful.

One such time was after a Sunday evening meeting when Katya had gone home to see to the children. Andrew and I found ourselves standing outside the Church building with Donka, Mariya and her friend, Mariya's sister Eva, and Jifca. – five of the poorest Church members. It was time to return Donka's hospitality.

"Let's go to the Restaurant" I suggested. Andrew nodded in agreement. Of course our guests had never been to a restaurant before in their lives! What a strange gathering of people we made: giggling teenagers; a deaf and dumb gypsy who could now hear; Donka, the provider of hospitality out of nothing; Andrew, a retired doctor, and myself. Only in the Kingdom of God can such groupings meet and enjoy fellowship together.

With the teenagers to entertain us, the evening was filled with laughter and joking. The Holy Spirit joined in too. We prayed for each other, we prophesied over each other, we blessed each other, and bathed in a joy that only comes from the throne of Heaven. These are rare and precious times when brothers and sisters are right with themselves, with each other and with God. King David even wrote a Psalm about it (Palm 133).

A few weeks later Donka suffered a heart attack from which she never recovered, and soon after went to be with the Lord. My last sight of her was enjoying Christian fellowship, full of the Holy Spirit and of Joy – a wonderful memory.

Donka's departing opened a new chapter in Mariya and Eva's lives. Their father returned from Greece to support them. An apartment was found for them by the local government. Their studies at school were uninterrupted.

Eva studies still to be a teacher. Mariya is at University, soon to graduate. Both are miracles I will never forget.

THE GYPSY CHURCH

The Church's appointment of the new Pastor proved a disaster.

The Pentecostal Church in Bulgaria has a clearly defined and almost legalistic system of appointing Church leaders. First, the Church, through its Council acting on behalf on the whole congregation, appoints the new Pastor. It is then the Pastor who has sole discretion to appoint two others to be his elders. If he is wise, the Pastor will use this opportunity to appoint according to the needs of the Church, bringing continuity with what has gone before.

The new Pastor at Katya's Church broke all these guidelines; and for the simple reason that he was *Turkish*! Because of a secondary status of Turkish people in Bulgaria, appointments of Turkish Pastors to a Bulgarian congregation are rare. Perhaps this was the reason he had not found a better appointment elsewhere. With wisdom these appointments can work. But this new and inexperienced Pastor *appointed two other Turkish Christians as elders.* In view of the vast experience and leadership of Peter and his fellow elder, this was a dreadful mistake, creating immense insult and hurt. To make matters worse, both Turkish men were from outside Troyan and virtually unknown to the Church. It was a Turkish takeover of a Bulgarian Church!

Nor did the problems stop there. These three men now imposed many changes in the Church and brushed aside all who objected. The Church was in chaos. Katya's family and other families stayed away in protest.

When I received news of what was happening I was deeply shocked. It seemed as if Satan was tearing the Church apart. I knew I had to stay clear. All I could do was pray.

It took eight months, and intervention from the Senior Pentecostal Pastor at Pleven, before the three Turkish men finally stepped down and left. Order was restored and somehow healing took place. But what happened next was quite extraordinary. The three Turkish men were invited by the Christian Gypsies to lead their Church; and this they did. The Turkish leaders' social standing gave them an authority which the Gypsies all recognised. The wisdom of the appointment was evident.

I'm sure all three men learnt a good deal in those eight short months. Yet the fallout from this continued. The Gypsies were banned from attending meetings at Katya's Church! They were also banned from meeting me! The Turkish leaders publicly denounced me as a "false prophet". But such encyclicals cut little ice with the Gypsies. They would make up their own minds.

Chapter Eight

DESPERATION

THE WOMAN WITH VITALIGO

After one Thursday evening meeting a young couple waited to see me.

" I've heard that you pray for people, and I want you to help me. It's my skin."

The young lady's name was Olga, a member of another Pentecostal Church in Troyan. She had a rare but striking skin problem called "Vitaligo". The skin dramatically discolours into large dark brown and white patches all over the body including hands and face. .

Our prayer time with Olga was arranged for an evening as Olga was one of a rare breed among the Troyan Christians—someone who had a good job! Her apartment was tidy and smartly furnished. With her was her fiancé, a bright and sympathetic young Christian man who was eager to help in any way he could. Everything was a success for Olga: her career; her forthcoming wedding plans; her home; her Christian friends – everything except her skin condition. I was strangely reminded of the story of General Naaman in the Old Testament. He too had everything going for him except for the secret hiding behind his armour – he was leprous (2 Kings 5:1). Olga's condition was not life threatening; but unlike Naaman's it could not be hidden.

Here was a young Christian woman, a spirit-filled Pentecostal Believer and committed member of her Church, who had been prayed for over and over again for her problem. But her prayers were never answered. If the skin problem had simply been the *problem*, it should have been healed years ago. From the start I felt I was looking at the *symptom* and not the problem. To discover this hidden problem I would have to listen to the Holy Spirit, and to Olga.

Olga had been married at a young age and went to live with her husband's family. She gave birth to a boy, and everything appeared to be going well. But when the little boy was eighteen months old he got sick and tragically died. Her husband was distraught, and grief turned to anger and the anger turned on Olga. Worse still, her mother-in-law also turned against Olga in a bitter and hateful way." It's your fault my grandson died. You are to blame." These spiteful accusations never abated, and in the heat of anger and bitterness Olga was threatened with a curse in revenge for the death of the child.

Somehow the marriage survived, and Olga had another baby boy. Again the boy grew normally and healthily until at around eighteen months tragedy struck again. Unbelievably, her second son also got sick and died suddenly. The anger and accusations were even more venomous. "It's all your fault. You are to blame. You are incapable of being a mother. You are a useless wife…" And this time her husband threw her out and divorced her.

Olga's life was in shreds, but it was the brown and white patches on her face and hands that were her hardest problem. It was her skin that marked out and publicly paraded her guilt, shame, rejection and failure in the past. With the promise of a new husband and a new life, this problem seemed to be tying her to the past, from which she found no escape. She was desperate to be rid of the past before starting her new life.

She had tried everything. She had received much prayer ministry, laying on of hands, and Christian support. She had been to doctors, skin specialists and herbalists. She had spent a fortune on every conceivable pill and potion. Nothing made the slightest difference. Like the woman who came to Jesus, "she had suffered a great deal under the care of many doctors and had spent all she had, yet instead of getting better she grew worse" (Mark 5:26). In absolute desperation she had come to see me.

Katya gently and lovingly put her arm around Olga for comfort and encouragement. Reminding herself of these tragic events had been difficult and painful. We all quietly prayed, calling on Jesus to come and heal. "Lord, teach us how to pray for Olga."

I asked Olga about her ex mother-in-law's threat of a curse. Had she carried this threat out? Olga had no means of knowing.

"Olga, in your spirit – deep down inside your heart – do you feel cursed?"

"Da" she replied.

"And did your skin problem start before or after your mother-in-law threatened a curse on you?

"It was after."

When praying with Christians it is important for they themselves to voice what has happened in their lives, lest we 'lead them on' and produce problems out of our own imagination. However, there are exceptions; and one is when someone is sharing very deep and painful trauma. To insist they speak it all out themselves often compounds the trauma. So there are times when, without leading them on, the Holy Spirit reveals the facts ahead of them; and all they need to say is a "yes" or "no" in response.

"Olga, when your first child died you were heartbroken."

"Da".

"And then your husband, instead of protecting and comforting you, blamed you. The guilt and shame you felt was multiplied, and it has tormented your heart ever since."

"Da".

"Because of the pain and trauma of losing your son, you were very vulnerable in your emotions. I believe a spirit of guilt and a spirit of shame entered your heart and spirit. How do you feel about this? Does that feel right with you?"

"Da. Da." responded Olga quietly, "the guilt and shame have ruled my life. I want to be free."

When the Holy Spirit counsels and those things hidden in darkness are exposed, God's peace comes among his people. For Olga victory was in sight. Jesus was shining a light into the darkness and revealing the truth. Satan no longer had a place to hide.

We began to pray.

It was important for Olga to forgive, and not hold back any bitterness. It was also important for Olga to repent of wrong reactions and attitudes and resentments built up in the heat of conflict. In my experience one true sign of repentance is when someone confesses their sin against people who have done the most wicked things to them. It is the Muslim who says "only God can forgive, I cannot"; the Christian prays "forgive us our trespasses as we forgive those who trespass against us."

Olga held nothing back, willingly repenting of her lack of love and patience, and resentments towards her mother-in-law. In my four years at Troyan, everyone who confessed their sins were healed, and those who claimed to be innocent went away empty. The Disciple John wrote that "If we claim to be without sin, we deceive ourselves and the truth is not in us. If we confess our sins, he is faithful and just, and will forgive us our sins and purify us from all unrighteousness." (1 John 1:8,9). Even the witch needed Olga's forgiveness. Indeed, if Olga had been unprepared to forgive the witch the curse could not have been broken – Satan would still have had a 'chain' around it.

With everything forgiven, there were no longer any 'chains' on the curse. I asked Olga's fiancée to break the curse in the name of Jesus.

He spoke out confidently and boldly: "I break this curse on you Olga in the name of Jesus. Amen."

Done!

Next we prayed deliverance of the spirits of guilt and shame.

Done!

After praying bad things out, it was now time to pray good things in. We prayed for love and peace and the restoration of her spirit.

Finally we prayed for the physical healing of Olga's skin problem.

Olga came to us with the symptom rather than the problem. She was healed because she was willing and determined to sort the problem behind the symptom. Many would have held back: "don't pray for that, pray for this!" But she was desperate, determined, repentant, and full of faith.

A few months later I returned to Troyan. Her skin was cleared and normal. Shortly after she married.

A CRIPPLED BABY

Not all the people who sought me out after Church meetings were Pentecostal believers. On one occasion I was surprised to meet a Ukranian man, who had come to Troyan with his wife in search of work and a better way of life. (They were to be disappointed, and after a year went back to their Ukrainian village).

They lived in a small shack at the bottom of someone's garden. This was near to the tiny rooms where Milena and her granddaughter held many home meetings. He was curious about the strange noises and singing that would emanate from their home. Often he would just come in, sit in the corner, and watch what was going on.

Soon after arriving in Troyan his young wife gave birth. When the baby was a few months old, it was discovered she had a crippled foot. The Bulgarian midwives are notoriously brutal. There are many cases of miscarriages after mothers attend prenatal checkups. Unlike England, there is no redress. The pre-natal care is free, but very basic, and many midwives are poorly trained.

The young Ukranian mother had had a difficult "breech" birth, and the baby came out feet first. The danger is always that permanent damage can be done to the babies ankles as it is dragged out. Such was the case here. The X-ray confirmed that the baby's right foot had been badly damaged. The father appealed for my help, showing me the X-ray evidence.

We went to their tiny makeshift home, accompanied by Minka and her granddaughter and all prayed.

On my next visit to Troyan I visited them again. The toddler's foot was now perfectly healthy. But instead of giving glory to Jesus, the Ukrainian mother insisted there had been no problem in the first place – even though the X-ray said otherwise.

A DYING MAN

The Ukrainian was not the only Orthodox Christian to come to me for help. At one morning meeting I noticed a lady in her sixties sitting at the back of the Church. She waited patiently afterwards to speak to me.

"My husband and I are not of this religion. We are from the Orthodox religion. My husband is very ill. The doctors say he is dying and they can do no more for him. Please come and pray for him."

I was so moved by the courage of this woman. She had come into what for her was an alien place of worship, with strange customs. She had risked being rejected because she was not of our 'religion'. She was both brave and desperate. The matter was urgent so Katya and I somehow found time that same afternoon.

The Orthodox lady welcomed us into her apartment, and we were led straight into the sitting room, where her husband lay on a makeshift bed. We introduced ourselves to the dying man, and then I asked his wife to leave. There are times when family are help and support in the prayer ministry, but when ministering to the dying, it is sometimes better for the patient to be alone. The emotions (seen or unseen) of relatives can inhibit a full and open response to Jesus.

The poor man was in agony, terrible agony. His condition was irreparable and terminal, but he was awake and able to hear and respond to us.

I was out of my depth. What could I do with an Orthodox man dying in great physical pain? I prayed, "Help Lord". These little cries for help came instinctively to me whenever I felt panic on the inside. I didn't know what to do or where to start! Katya also felt uneasy. We had no idea where this man was in Christ, and we were not prepared to pray some pretty or formal prayers that we knew would be of little help.

I prayed again: "Lord, what do I do?" as I held the man's hand. A lot can be conveyed through the holding of a dying man's hand: confidence, assurance, comfort, compassion, love and tenderness. From what is communicated in that touch can discourage or encourage response and faith.

We both quietly prayed aloud in tongues, and a lovely sense of peace began filtering into the room. The man was untroubled by this gift of tongues. Far from being offended by it, many *dying* people respond positively to what they sense is something from Heaven, because that's where most dying people want to go.

I cannot pray for people's needs without using this most precious gift from Heaven. Of course, the gift can be abused, but the few times Christians experience that should never discourage our use of it. When praying for others there are so many times when I have no idea how to pray. Praying quietly in tongues continues a dialogue with Heaven, when my mind runs out of words and ideas. It is the Holy Spirit praying through me, sorting out the hidden obstacles I am unaware of. The Holy Spirit finds the words I cannot find because *He* knows what to pray for. Many times the 'atmosphere' changes within minutes of praying in tongues. Peace and clarity come into confused and distressing situations.

God's peace came into that room. Perhaps the angels came too, though I didn't see any. But clarity suddenly came into my mind with the words:

"First the spiritual, then the emotional, and then the physical."

One test of whether a Word from God is really from God or just from one's own imagination, is one's reaction to it. In this case I was quite surprised – even shocked. I would have wanted to settle the dying man's pain first (the physical). How could he respond to ministry for other things when in such pain? I was surprised at what God had said. How could I surprise myself if these were my own imaginings? No, this was from the Lord. God's priorities are different from ours. We are a society obsessed with every conceivable trapping of well being for our physical bodies. God is far more concerned with our spiritual well being.

"First the spiritual......"

I reminded the dying Orthodox man about the ministry of the Priest in his Church. With my early years in the Anglo-Catholic branch of the Church of England I was familiar with the principles of priesthood as understood by the Orthodox. I could use language he understood. I reminded him of his Orthodox Priest, appointed by God to listen to sin in confession and pronounce forgiveness.

"Da" he responded.

Then I told him about our Great High Priest, Jesus the Son of God, "a merciful and faithful high priest in service to God" (Hebrews 2:17). We can come to Jesus, make confession and receive forgiveness. "Let us then approach the throne of grace with confidence, so that we may receive mercy and find grace to help us in time of need." (Hebrews 4:16).

"Do you understand?

"Da."

"I want you to picture Jesus as your great High Priest, having far more authority than even the most senior priests in your Church. Can you do this?"

"Da."

"I want you to tell him all the bad things you've ever done. The Holy Spirit will help you. I want you to speak aloud. Katya and I will pray aloud as you do this. Is that OK?"

"Da"

With little encouragement he began speaking. We prayed in tongues. I couldn't understand a word he was saying but in my spirit it felt as if a dam had burst and it was all pouring out. We continued praying aloud. "Is it coming out?" I quietly asked Katya. "Yes" she replied. We prayed non-stop until he had finished. It was as if our praying in tongues were 'oiling the wheels' of his confession.

"Is that everything?" I asked him.

"Da".

I could not but be impressed by the sheer determination of this man to find peace with God. I now did something I hadn't done before in Troyan. Having quickly gone into the kitchen and got a few drops of cooking oil from his wife, I took a little of the oil on my thumb. "In the name of the Father and of the Son and the Holy Spirit I pronounce you forgiven and set free from your sins." With each member of the Trinity I used the oil to mark a small cross on his forehead. (See James 5:13-16).

As a Priest in the Church of England I had been ordained for this ministry. But we often forget that there is Biblical authority for *all of us* who are members of the Kingdom of Heaven to do this. We are all being built up "to be a holy priesthood" (1 Peter 2:5). For some there is difficulty with us *pronouncing* forgiveness. But this is little different from us saying when praying with others "God has forgiven you". "Pronouncing" is more authoritative, the same authority the Holy Spirit gives when "commanding" spirits to go and "breaking" curses. "Pronouncing" forgiveness is a confirming of what God has done: a speaking out of the assurance we have from His Word: "If we confess our sins, he is faithful and just and will forgive us our sins." (1 John 1:9).

"......then the emotional..."

I explained to the dying man how Jesus died on the Cross to forgive our sins but also to free us from fears and worries and anxieties or anything else that troubled us. The Bible encourages us to "cast all your anxiety on Him because He cares for you." (I Peter 5:7). Do you understand?

"Da."

"Have you got any anxieties or fears?"

To my surprise he answered "Ne." I paused. He was responding honestly and not just politely agreeing with everything I said. It reminded me how problematic language can be; how one word can convey different meanings with different people. In Bulgaria it was doubly difficult as Katya had to struggle to find the appropriate words in translation. I decided on a different word to express the same idea.

"Are you *worried* about anything?"

"Da".

I then encouraged him to speak out all his worries as we prayed with him. I explained how we can take these worries, like a bag of rubbish, to the Cross and leave them at Jesus' feet. He responded positively to this. It was amazing that an Orthodox man could respond so quickly to counselling which Christians in Evangelical Churches might take years to respond to.

"......then the physical."

After this it was a straightforward task to ask the Lord to take away his pain. Katya slowly and tenderly translated, and the man repeated after me:

"Lord Jesus, you are the King of Kings and Lord of Lords......I thank you for forgiving me...... and setting me free from all my fears... ... Come now and fill my heart with your presence...... Fill my heart with your love... ... Fill my heart with your peace... ... Take away all the pain in my body... ... and bring me into your eternal Kingdom. Amen."

Peace came on all three of us. Within minutes this dying man, who not long earlier had been in agony, was fast asleep; freed of everything that had been troubling him. Two days later he died.

His wife was anxiously waiting in the kitchen, hoping for some physical miracle and her husband to walk in. We never prayed for that. There was a divide between what she wanted and what the Lord wanted. She wanted him well and walking round the house again. *Her prayers had not been answered.*

But his prayers **had** been answered. He needed forgiveness and reconciliation with God. He needed to be free from all his fears. He needed peace in his heart and mind and body. What she wanted she couldn't have, but what he *needed* in Christ Jesus, he cried out for and received. God was teaching me the difference between 'wants' and 'needs'. I was learning why some prayers go unanswered.

We *have* to be in tune with God's purposes when praying with the terminally sick. "There is a time for everything, and a season for every activity under heaven: a time to be born and a time to die." (Ecclesiastes 3:1,2)

BOBBY

A young Gypsy mother came to see me with her three-year-old son, Bobby. She was a Christian whom Katya had known for many years. She had been a member of Katya's Church before marrying a Muslim Gypsy husband. Now she was living with her husband's family in a small Gypsy community a short distance outside the town. Physically isolated from her Christian friends, she had stopped attending Church to avoid conflict with her new family. But her faith was still very real.

Bobby was suffering from a rare type of kidney failure, and she begged me to come and visit her home.

We arrived to a cool though not unfriendly reception. The Muslim Gypsies were embarrassed that they had to call on a Christian to pray for their needs. I resolved to do all I could to befriend and get alongside them.

Her husband gave me a warm greeting and we entered their tiny house. She told us their story. Bobby had been sickly and ill from being a baby. About a year earlier, when only two years old, he had been referred by the Hospital to a specialist clinic in Sophia. The clinic had diagnosed a rare kidney condition in the little boy, which I later discovered was known as **glomerulonephritis**. It is an autoimmune deficiency; or, in simpler terms, the filter system of the kidneys ceases to function. The disease is often fatal in small children whose bodies are not strong enough to fight back and recover.

Bobby's mother had done everything she could, making many long and exhausting journeys to Sofia to keep appointments at the City Hospital's Nephrology Clinic. They had spent all their money on travel and medicine, and were now desperate.

The child's failing health was compounded by three other factors:

First, he was allergic to cow's milk and other dairy products, which deprived him of an important source of protein. He was surviving almost exclusively on Soya milk.

Second, the family's financial resources were spent on travel to Sofia; and what food they could buy was of poor quality. A good diet was essential for his survival.

Third, what medicine was available was of little benefit.

Bobby had been given 3 to 6 months to live. He was deteriorating in weight and strength. They were fighting a losing battle.

I had discovered that there were a number of examples of first-born sons in Troyan suffering unusual illness. Among the Gypsies, unofficially arranged marriages were commonplace. It might be assumed for years who was marrying whom. Parents and families would plan and scheme, with their daughters traded almost as efficiently as their horses! So when an expectation over a future marriage was betrayed and long-standing promises of betrothal broken, revenge was commonplace.

The most severe form of revenge was the curse, which could be used to harm the person betraying a pledge; but it could, and sometimes was, used to harm the first-born son. By this, not only was the marriage and family punished, but the mother would suffer lifelong grief. For us brought up in Christian Britain such evil is beyond our credibility; but in Troyan (and other Bulgarian communities) it was happening.

I tried very gently to approach this subject and enquire if there had been any arguments or strong objections to their marriage or threats of revenge. (As a Christian she would not have been the first candidate for marriage). Bobby's mother stayed silent, and the father shrugged his shoulders. Had they heard that I had prayed against curses? Was there a dark family secret they would not disclose? This was not an easy situation. Bobby's Muslim father seemed restless and uncomfortable. As such his priority was honour of the family, rather than the truth. Perhaps this was the reason I sensed hostility in the initial welcome. Was I posing a threat to them in some way?

We prayed for the child, but I felt very uneasy. Was I not simply praying for the symptom and not the problem?

After we prayed Bobby's mother shared more information about her son's medical condition. It was as if she knew little would come of the prayers, and wanted to explain the real reason I had been invited. She had been told of a new medicine that had been developed for this problem, but it was very expensive. Only the Clinic in Sofia had access to it.

Two days later we all travelled to Sofia to see. We were able to meet the Professor of Nephrology at the City Hospital; but our hopes of getting help were soon shattered. There was no medicine available. I persisted.

There must be some of the new medicine *somewhere*! Finally the Professor capitulated and handed me the Email Address of the Head of Research at Novartis, the giant Swiss Pharmaceutical Company.

The following day I left Troyan for home, promising Bobby's mother I would try to help. But what could I do?

Within thirty minutes of arriving home in Derbyshire I had emailed Novartis. I explained who I was and a little of what I was doing in Troyan. (The fact that I was married to a family doctor certainly helped.) I made it clear that the Bulgarian family were Gypsies, and Bobby had an allergy to dairy products and poor diet.

I could scarcely believe it when the reply returned within 48 hours. Novartis promised to dispatch one year's supply of the new drug (cost £1500) for free! The only conditions were that the Hospital in Troyan should supervise the administration of it (it is lethal taken in the wrong dosage), and that a three-monthly examination report by the Sophia Nephrology Clinic be sent to Novartis. All was agreed. The medicine arrived at my home two weeks later, and the following week I was back in Troyan!

I later discussed with my wife what had taken place. She agreed that such expensive and toxic medicines are *never* handed over to individuals; less still, someone with no medical background! It is only ever from clinic to clinic.

The impossible happened, and the medicine saved his life.

Chapter Nine

A SECOND PENTECOSTAL CHURCH

After my first two years of travelling to Bulgaria, I was noticing changes in the familiar travel route from Sofia to Troyan. Arranging the Hertz hire car from Sofia Airport was easy. I knew my way around the City and how to get to the Christian Bookshop. I had learnt the local shortcut from the Airport to the Troyan road, which avoided the City Centre. (Signposts in Sophia City seemed almost nonexistent, as the country had little experience of foreigners driving around getting lost!) I had learnt to avoid the notorious potholes that could snap an axel like a matchstick. Now they were being meticulously filled up.

The super highway from Sofia through the mountains to the Black Sea was painstakingly being constructed. Huge state-of-the-art bridges up to one kilometre in length were being built, spanning the narrow valleys and dramatically cutting journey time. From a gruelling four hours in my first bus from Sophia, Troyan was now little over two hours away by car.

Tourism was coming, and the government was waking up to its enormous economic potential. Bulgaria had everything for the Western family looking for a holiday. It was cheap, safe, and welcoming. The summer climate rivalled the Mediterranean; and Bulgaria had a trump card—the wonderful Black Sea with the summer temperature of a warm bath!

Life in Troyan, however, remained unchanged. The tourists sped passed the Troyan turn-off, with its little missable sign on the highway. Although only a 25 km detour, the little mountain town might as well have been 250 km. away. The coming tourist boom held few benefits for Troyan.

But there were some changes. Vasil and Katya had a new home, a small house about 200 metres from Katya's parents. They had prayed and prayed for a home of their own, but waited for the right one to be available. This one was perfect. It had a garage right by the roadside, tailor-made for Vasil to develop his new business servicing cars. The tiny single storey house had a small annex at the back, with two rooms and bathroom – perfect to fulfil Katya's desire to offer hospitality.

Another change that occurred around this time was contact with the other Pentecostal Church in Troyan. I had heard of this already through ministering to Olga, but had no subsequent contact with them. My commission from the Lord had always been to "go to *the* Church in Troyan" and not "a church". I was interested in meeting with all the Churches. I expected an invitation from this other Pentecostal Church, but it never came.

Later I would discover some of the reasons for this. The two Churches had formed from a 'split' in the original Troyan Pentecostal Church. This had taken place in the 1920's. The division of the original Church had been very bitter. Even after seventy years there were wounds among some of the older members that hadn't healed. Sadly, some of this resentment had gone down the generations. Only the teenagers of both Churches appeared sufficiently disinterested in the past to be able to meet together and share fellowship.

My only experience of these believers was Olga, a young Christian woman full of faith and love for the Lord, and of the Holy Spirit. With Christians like her, why the continued suspicion and distrust?

After nearly two and a half years a door finally opened.

Katya and I were walking through the Town Square on the way to an appointment when a group of young adults passed us. Katya said "hello" to one of them.

"They're from the other Church," Katya casually remarked.

In a knee-jerk reaction I went after them.

"Hello" I said deliberately," It's nice to meet you all."

Their response was unexpected.

"Oh!" one of them replied, "we didn't think you wanted to see us."

After spending two and a half years responding to every invitation I was given, I was shocked.

"Oh yes, I would *love* to meet you all. Please invite me."

With that an invitation to one of their homes was hastily arranged. Finally a door was opening into the other Church.

The evening meal Katya and I were invited to was filled with young Christians in their 20's and early 30's. This Church appeared to be overflowing with young adults. I was delighted to be in such company. Here were young enthusiastic hearts for the Lord, the seeds of revival; and among them were Christo and Maggie.

Christo's parents were to his Church what Katya's were to hers – key leadership families that went back to the split. Both Christo and Maggie had a University education, and Maggie had studied English. She had sufficient command of the language to be able to understand and translate. In that one evening I was introduced to them and invited to their home. The Lord had brought me into the heart of the other Church.

Christo and Maggie were remarkably open about the strengths and failings of their Church, and the more they explained the more I understood the reasons for not only the original split, but the continued mistrust and suspicion.

Christo's Church was what we would call today a 'signs and wonders' Church. It met not only to worship and learn from God's Word, but also to receive the gifts of the Holy Spirit through Tongues and Prophecies and other gifts. This emphasis on the gifts rather than the Giver can have great dangers. Often Christians, under pressure for something to happen, 'manufacture' manifestations of the Holy Spirit. God is expected to 'perform' every Sunday morning whether He wants to or not!

But a bigger problem still, is the subtle attraction such services have for extroverts, attention-seekers, and people with religious spirits. In an 'anything goes' atmosphere it is not unknown for non-Christians to come in pretending to speak in the name of Jesus.

I asked about their Pastor and how he kept order in the meeting. The answer was gentle and non-judgmental, but what they seemed to imply was that, after thirty years at this Church he had lost the plot! Strong-willed women, intent on performing their signs and wonders on a Sunday morning, had taken over. His only authority lay in the making of new rules and regulations. While outwardly appearing to have freedom, the Church had fallen into a terrible legalism. For example everyone had to kneel for prayer. Standing up was not acceptable. In home meetings they curled up like hedgehogs to pray, which appeared more Islamic than Christian. The latest rule, Maggie told me, was concerning the length of women's hair, which could be no shorter than shoulder length! There were rules for almost everything; and compliance was expected of the Church members. To break a rule was a sin; and had to be dealt with as such. The freedom that Jesus brings had been replaced by a Pharisaic system of laws. The Gospel had been turned upside down.

But there was another, even more disturbing aspect to this Church. This was its teaching on conversion. The test of any Church is its teaching regarding how to become a Christian. Among the counterfeit teachings we often hear in England are…

…'If you were born a Christian then you are a Christian'.

…'If you were christened as a baby you are a Christian'.

…'If you join a church you are a Christian'.

…'If you say your prayers and read your Bible you are a Christian'.

…'If you do your best and believe in God you are a Christian'.

There are so many examples of counterfeit teaching on what makes you a Christian. But Christo's Church had a new and completely unexpected one.:

…"Baptism in the Holy Spirit *makes* you a Christian."

Here was a devious confusion. Christo's Church taught that conversion takes place when someone is Baptised in the Holy Spirit. This was a subtle but significant change from the New Testament, which teaches that Baptism in the Holy Spirit is received at or after conversion.

But there was more. The Church taught that the proof of Baptism of the Holy Spirit was the speaking of two or three words in tongues. An unbeliever could go through some form of ministry and prayer, and afterwards, if they uttered just two words in tongues they would be accepted by the congregation as a Born-again Christian.

Now I was beginning to understand why Katya tended to distance herself from this Fellowship. It wasn't bitterness from the past, but deception in the present.

At the same time, I was meeting soundly converted and mature Christians from this Church. Olga was full of faith and the Holy Spirit and had come through a remarkable healing. Christo and Maggie were wonderful believers, earnestly praying for revival. They grieved over these deep-seated problems in their own Church, and were constantly wondering if they should leave. It was Christo and Maggie and the younger adults in their church who annually holidayed at the Bulgarian equivalent of Spring Harvest (an inter-denominational camp for all ages) every year.

Many of the young adults in Christo's Church had been converted in a mini-revival that had happened in Troyan in the months following the fall of the Berlin Wall. At that time the stigma and penalties for being Pentecostal Christians were eased and teenagers were looking to Western thought and ideas as a foundation for their lives. Some searched the Bible for the first time and found answers! Around thirty young people in their late teens and early twenties were saved. Many were still in Christo's Church.

CHRISTO AND MAGGIE'S HOSPITALITY

Christo and Maggie became instant friends; and they were eager to offer their home both for hospitality and accommodation. They lived with Christo's parents and younger brother, and had a small but comfortable section of the house to themselves and their two-year-old boy, Alexander.

Christo's Church, for all its many problems, was still part of the Body of Christ in Troyan. So although I felt some in Katya's Church would be apprehensive, I knew it was right for me to be here. I decided to accept their offer of hospitality. Whenever I came alone to Troyan I would stay at Katya's new home; but if Andrew accompanied me he would stay with Katya, while I would go to Christo's. By these arrangements and actions I was demonstrating that *both* congregations were part of the Church in Troyan. And there were some benefits. The teenagers of both churches met more regularly together; and Katya and Maggie also began meeting together in fellowship.

The evenings I spent at Christo and Maggie's were full of questions and more questions, and neither worried if these went late into the night. Having waited six months from one visit to another, they had many questions ready waiting for me. Neither were they afraid to "speak the truth in love." Many of the lessons in this book they 'squeezed' out of me! They were hungry for the Kingdom of God. Just as Katya had a broader Christian vision through her experience of the Church in America, so Christo and Maggie's experiences at the Summer Camps broadened their vision.

"One day there will be a home cell group here" I thought.

Like many other young men in Troyan, Christo tragically found himself out of work. In desperation he had applied to one of the few places where jobs were vacant – the Prison! There were two vacancies for junior guards, and Christo had survived hundreds of applicants to be on the final shortlist of nine.

That week I intervened:

"Colonel Marin," I began hesitantly, " I have never in my life asked a special favour such as the one I am going to ask. And I don't intend to mention the subject again."

"Da?"

He instantly became more serious and concentrated. Although Katya translated faithfully every word I spoke to him, I now realised that his English was very good and he could understand much of what I was saying. .

"I understand you are about to appoint two new warders from a short list of nine." He was surprised by my inside information. "One of those on the short list is a man called Christo. I want you to know that I've known Christo personally for almost a year; and I also know his wife and his parents. He is a gifted Christian man, a hard-working young man with integrity and honesty. If you appoint him he will not let you down."

Marin made no comment, and nothing further was ever said.

Three months later Christo got the job. Six months after that he rose to the rank of senior warden. A righteous Prison Director appointing a man of integrity. God now had his man on the inside.

FROM NEEDS TO WANTS

The opening up of contacts with the other Church was not the only change taking place. The motives of those coming to see me were changing. For the first two years there was repentance in their requests. Most were longstanding Christians that Katya knew well. They brought problems which they had prayed about for a long time, often years. They were full of faith, they were desperate, and they were willing to lay everything at the feet of Jesus.

Gradually things changed, and the people seeing me more and more simply wanted an easy solution to their problem – the quick fix! Having heard the rumour—'Pastor Allan can fix it'—they came to me without that heart-centred willingness to submit to Jesus.

I prayed to the Lord about this……"help me understand what is happening."…and the answer came back: "They are more concerned with what they want rather than what they need. I am concerned with what they *need*." Paul reminded the Christians in Philippi at the end of his letter that "my God will meet all your *needs* according to his glorious riches in Christ Jesus" (Phil 4:19).

I was still learning important lessons. I had learnt the importance of distinguishing problem from symptom; and how God is always concerned with the problem. Once He has removed that, the symptom goes too! When the broken arm is mended, the pain disappears.

Now I was learning the difference between 'wants' and 'needs'. Most parents understand it all too well. Children want a packet of crisps but *need* a healthy meal; they want to bounce around in the car, but *need* to be strapped in by the seatbelt; they want to stay up late watching TV, but *need* a good night's sleep. Every good parent is primarily concerned with their child's needs. So it is with our Father in Heaven.

Chapter Ten

THE IMPORTANCE OF REPENTANCE

A MAN INTO WITCHCRAFT.

It was after the time I had made friends with Christo and Maggie, but before I was fully aware of the confusion and deception among them, that a man from their Church came to see me. He arrived with his married daughter and friend.

We relaxed and talked awhile, but once I began enquiring about the man's problems things started to get confused. I felt the things he was sharing had been shared with many others before me. He told me in great detail about his past experiences and involvement with various occult activities; of the sacrifices of chickens and more sinister involvement with so-called 'black' witchcraft (all witchcraft is 'black'). He appeared to take great delight in explaining the details – as if still fascinated by it.

As Katya and I listened it was obvious he had been deeply involved, not as a spectator or customer; he had practised witchcraft himself! What was less clear was what his problem was now. As a converted Christian he would have repented of these things and received forgiveness and restoration a long time ago. I was getting more and more confused as he spoke about his past. Usually the Holy Spirit gives me clarity when praying for someone, but not this time.

I asked him if he was still troubled by his past, and we prayed through repentance and restoration. But there was no inner witness of either a contrite heart or the Holy Spirit bringing peace. I was beginning to think he had come more to test my 'magic' and see how 'powerful' I was.

When the three of them left I was still confused. These were key people in Christo's Church, and I respected them for that. His daughter especially was involved in various ministries in the Church. It was only the following day, while praying about it all, that the Lord spoke to me: "did you test to see if he was a Christian?" Immediately I realised what a terrible mistake I had made. No wonder nothing seemed to happen when we prayed. No wonder there was no Holy Spirit witness to the 'repentance'. It had all been a charade to test me out! I had learnt an important lesson.

THE TEENAGER WITH A STRAPPED BACK

A sixteen-year-old teenage boy came to see me after Church. Unusually, he didn't come to the meeting, but had found out the timings and came in a few minutes after the meeting finished.

He had had a severe back problem for many years, a very rare and unusual occurrence for a healthy young man. Strapped around his waist was an eight-inch (25cm) wide brace. He seemed very impatient for me to 'get on with it'. Possibly he had been told about the 'miracle worker' at the Pentecostal Church. He was not a Christian and had little idea what I was about. He simply wanted a quick fix! He wanted me to solve his problem. But I wondered if I was looking at the symptom rather than the problem. I needed a private time with him to ask questions. A 'quick fix' was what I couldn't do.

I *never* pray for healing without asking questions. That is as irresponsible as a doctor writing prescriptions without asking questions. The 'quick fix prayer' and 'pat on the head' for serious and complicated problems never solves anything; rather, it brings dishonour to the Lord. It is **His** ministry we are engaged with and not our own. *We* may feel a little better after a quick fix prayer, but what about the feelings of the person who leaves with nothing? How do they think and feel? Simply that God isn't interested; God doesn't care; God cannot do anything; or God's just not there!

There was no time available for this young man. My programme was full, and his predicament looked complicated. Why, for example, after all these years had the doctors at the Hospital been unsuccessful? It 'smelled' of something much more sinister, but there was no time now.

Dozens of those I had prayed for in Troyan had patiently and faithfully waited the six months for my return. But in that waiting, I know many had prayed and prepared, had searched their hearts and got themselves ready to do 'business' with God. That was one reason why so many amazing things happened. They were *ready* for ministry. I never once failed to keep my promise to see them the next time. Sadly this young man would have to wait too.

Perhaps others had sent him for a 'quick fix'. He seemed very unsure and out of place, almost as if he hadn't wanted to come. But I wanted to encourage him as much as I could. I took him to a quiet corner, and spoke gently to him:

"When Jesus, the Son of God, was on the earth and healed the sick, they came to Him and knelt at His feet. They cried out in repentance and declared Jesus the Lord of their lives. This is what Jesus is asking of you. I want you to ask Jesus to help you. I want you to cry out to Jesus in the quiet of your own room and ask for help. I want you to come and see me next time I am in Troyan. I promise you will be at the top of my list; and I will pray for you then.

He smiled half-heartedly. It was not what he had been expecting. But to have prayed for him at that point would have dishonoured the Lord. *We should never pray just in case it might work*! Our prayers should be in Him and sanctioned by His Spirit. Having challenged him I then prayed for him:

"Lord bless this young man. Lord reveal yourself to him. Lord open his heart to you. Lord prepare a time for us to meet again."

It was not difficult for outsiders to know when I was coming to Troyan. The dates were publicised in the church, and news gets round. Those who want to know, find out. How desperate was this young man? I passionately hoped he would see me again; but sadly he didn't.

THE ELDERLY LADY WITH A THROAT PROBLEM

One Sunday morning an elderly lady asked for my prayers.

"What is the problem?" I asked.

"It's my throat." She replied.

"What's wrong with it?

"I don't know" she insisted.

"What does the doctor say the problem is?"

"I don't go to doctors. Jesus is all I need. I want you to pray for it."

"It's important for me to know what the doctor says" I gently insisted.

"Oh, I'm not going to the doctor!"

I persisted, a little more firmly; "I want you to go to the doctor; and next time I come to Troyan I promise I'll pray for you."

By now she was getting a little irate: "I don't need doctors. I only need Jesus!"

My reply to that shocked her, and will probably shock others as well ;

"If you won't go to the doctor, then I cannot pray for you."

With that she walked off, disgusted!

I felt terrible, but in my spirit I knew the Holy Spirit had given me wisdom. I had never seen her before and had no idea about her religious background. I looked at Katya.

"Don't worry" she said, almost dismissively, " she has often come and tried to make trouble in the Church. She was only wanting to avoid paying the doctor's fee!" How important it is to listen to the Holy Spirit and have His guidance. When guided by the Lord our words and actions can be different from what our rational minds, and rational friends, would have advised. But God knows best!

In all these cases of the man involved with witchcraft, the teenager with back problems and the elderly lady with a throat problem, God had been teaching me important lessons. Don't assume a member of a Church is a Christian! Don't be pressured into praying before it's time to pray. Don't succumb to the pressure of the moment to do what is expected – be led by the Holy Spirit! All three were vital lessons that I would need when I met to pray with Maya.

MAYA

Maya was 26 years old; an educated young woman completely devoted to God. For seven years she had been a youth leader, teaching the teenagers the Christian faith. She was a member of Christo's Church, and had asked Katya and me for help.

When she began to tell us her story we were amazed at how the Grace of God had protected and upheld her life. She had suffered from almost every conceivable childhood problem – rejection, lack of love, abuse, bullying, insecurity, fears of various things, anorexia, bad dreams... The list was endless. We didn't know where to start! Nor did the problems end with her teenage years. She still suffered from anorexia, sleepless nights, self-rejection, lack of confidence, and low self-esteem. She was still full of fears. In 24 years of praying for people I had never encountered anyone with so many problems! Every one of her problems would, in normal circumstances, have been a 'two hour job'! I had no idea where to begin.

We needed help, and began to ask for it. After a few minutes of quietly praying, the Lord said to me: "is she in Christ?" As a teacher of the Gospel in the Church before my own conversion, I knew this was entirely possible. And I was reminded of the utter confusion in Christo's Church over what constituted conversion.

Jesus warned His Disciples not to judge others; that is, not to be judgmental towards them. But it is easy to confuse being judgmental with the need on occasion to test if someone is really Born Again. The two are different. Jesus warns us about being judgemental; but Paul positively instructs the Church to "test everything" (1 Thess. 5:21).

Testing whether someone is Born Again by the Spirit of God is not difficult; neither does it have to be embarrassing or threatening. It is simply a matter of asking them to share their testimony and *listening* to them.

Every single believer who is a member of the Kingdom of Heaven has a testimony to share. I remember one sister once sharing with me that as long as she could ever remember she had had a love for and relationship with Jesus. What a testimony! Not every testimony names places, dates and times; but the great majority do. For most of us we can never forget because the day of our conversation is the single most important day of our lives. So to ask for a testimony is not an irksome task, but an opportunity to share and to listen to a most wonderful story.

And at the heart of that testimony should **always** be a personal relationship with the person of Jesus. We should always be cautious about any testimony that centres only on going to meetings!

Maya began to share her testimony.

"I started going to the Church and then they prayed for me to speak in tongues. I managed to speak two words in tongues and I was told I was a Christian."

Her testimony was cold and clinical. It seemed well rehearsed, as if she recited exactly the same words to anyone who enquired. Katya and I, without speaking a word to each other, both knew we were at the heart of Maya's problem. She had given us a comprehensive catalogue of her troubles. She *wanted* us to fix her troubles, but what she *needed* was Jesus in her life! All the troubles were but the *symptom*, the **problem** was that she "was separate from Christ... Without hope and without God in the world." (Ephesians 2:12).

Sometimes the most difficult people to bring to Christ are those convinced, through the doctrine of their own churches, that they already are Christians. It is a battle between David and Goliath; between a lone voice speaking through the power of the Holy Spirit, and the mighty tradition and authority of that Church. It is the same battle whether it is the Church of Rome, or a tiny Pentecostal Church in Troyan.

We asked Maya about her own personal relationship with Jesus, and it was obvious to all of us, herself included, how utterly lacking this was. Maya was hungry for the Lord, but had never really repented and asked Jesus into her life. She had simply been led through a religious ritual, and accepted what she had been told. How many are led astray in this way!

Katya and I knew we were walking on eggshells! We were beginning to challenge the foundations on which she had built her life. We needed the Holy Spirit to be gentle, loving, supportive and encouraging. Moreover, there was a battle being fought in Heaven for Maya's soul.

Eventually she was prepared to come to repentance and ask Jesus into her life. In practice this would mean more than confession of sins, or even surrendering her life. It would mean the renouncing and handing over of all 'spiritual' gifts to Jesus – even ones sincerely believed to be given by the Holy Spirit. Everything had to go.

It would have been easy to have made a small compromise. 'Soften the blow and make it easier for her' says the Devil! "Alright," I could so easily have said, " you can keep your gift of tongues. It's not a problem because Jesus will give you a better one!" But that would be to make a deal with God. *Compromising His principles compromises His holiness.* **God never does deals!** As gently as we could, we had to insist on everything being surrendered, including all that she had held dear for many years as her special God-given spiritual gifts.

Maya was unwilling to surrender her gift of 'tongues'. For 20 minutes she offered every argument and smokescreen to avoid doing this. I encouraged her all I could:

"When you make Jesus the Lord of your life you have to trust that He has the very best for you in everything, including spiritual gifts. Hand it to Him, and if it truly is the gift He has for you He'll give it right back to you. Sometimes when we become Christians Jesus touches the most precious thing we hold dear. Sometimes this is money, sometimes family or children. For me it was my ministry as a Priest. It was the most important thing in my life. It was what God had 'called' me to be from the age of sixteen. It was the only thing I ever did or wanted to do. But I had to surrender it back to Him. In the same way He is calling you to surrender your gift of tongues because He knows it is the most precious thing you have. You have to trust Him and make Him your Lord."

There was more silence, followed by more theological objections and red herrings. I kept her clearly focussed on the one and only issue. A few minutes later, with what seemed an insurmountable standoff, I challenged her in a way I have never done before or since:

"I have to go in fifteen minutes. You have fifteen minutes to come to Jesus at the Cross – on His terms."

She knew exactly what I meant.

More arguments and excuses followed.

"You've ten minutes..."

More arguments and excuses.

"I'm leaving in three minutes..."

With that she fell down on her knees and cried out to Jesus. It didn't need any translation. She prayed and cried and prayed and cried. Everything was pouring out. The Holy Spirit was witnessing with our spirits to what an amazing miracle was happening before our eyes. Katya and I just prayed and prayed and prayed. For ten or fifteen minutes came this unending stream of repentance. We were all in tears. A dam of pride and religious self-satisfaction had burst. Real repentance had come. It was truly wonderful!

When she was finally finished and completely exhausted, I asked her if she wanted to be Baptised in the Holy Spirit.

"Da"

This time we all stood up before the King: and we prayed. Katya in Bulgarian and myself in English. We prayed for everything. She had completely emptied herself before the Cross, and now came the wonderful privilege of praying every blessing, gift and grace into a new Christian's life.

Tongues came too, and it poured out of her. Not two measly 'words', but an overflowing language from Heaven in praise of our God and King.

Six months later Maya came to Troyan especially to see me. She was full of the Joy of the Lord. Her face beamed. I asked her about the fears and other problems that had been dominating her life.

"Oh, they've gone!"

"What?" I asked rather incredulously. "All of them?"

"Da. *All of them*!"

Chapter Eleven

MY LAST VISIT TO TROYAN

My last visit came as unexpectedly as my first. In every respect it was as all the others. The dates were planned in advance. The accommodation was arranged. The sermons were prepared. The list of people waiting to see me was well prayed over. The Church was looking forward to seeing me again. There was no hint that this visit would be different from the others.

But two apparently trivial things made this visit different. One of Jifca's friends, a mature Christian Gypsy, met me with something urgent she felt she had to share with me. She spoke quite nervously, but deliberately:

"Brother Allan, I want to say to you with love in my heart that you are doing more harm than good."

The words stunned me for a moment. This was unexpected. At the same time it was said without anger or bitterness or malice. It had been a hard message for her to share with me, and it had been shared lovingly and gently. I heard the Holy Spirit in those words, and I thanked her for being brave enough to share something so difficult with me.

What was going on? I asked the Lord for help. It would have been difficult to share this with the Church because it had been a Gypsy who had spoken these words, and I didn't want the Gypsies to be somehow blamed on my departure.

Confirmation that God was speaking to me came at the very end of the Sunday evening meeting. Everyone who had requested prayer had been prayed for. For the first time in four and a half years *there was no-one left to pray for.* My work had come to an end.

There has never been any regret in making that my last visit. It would have been so easy to continue year after year, getting a buzz from a reputation of past blessings. It would have been 'something positive' to do in my old age!

But I know the Holy Spirit. His works of Power are often for a reason and for a season. I wanted to be in His purposes and not mine. The 'season' of my work had come to an end.

It is often easier to recognise the Lord opening a door, than shutting it. When doors open the confirmations and encouragement can be very strong. Too often the same ear does not listen when the door closes. Ministries continue long after their sell by dates. Often we find ourselves living on the successes of the past, when God has moved on.

The writer of Ecclesiastes tells us (Chapter 3) that there is, in God's sovereign plan, a season for everything. The older I get, the more I understand the profound wisdom of this. My work in Troyan had always been planned for a season – no more! It was a wonderful season, full of blessing, encouragement, miracle and healing. It was a season of instruction.

MY FINAL SERMON

I found myself preaching my final sermon without realising it. Only after that Sunday evening service, when the queue finished, would I know for sure my work was at an end. I still have the scrap of paper on which I wrote five headings, in English and Bulgarian—my final sermon.

My talks to Katya's Church had started very gently, with teaching on how to become a Christian and the importance of being Baptised in the Holy Spirit. The talks gradually became more and more challenging: the need for repentance; the need for reconciliation and healing among the Churches; the need for personal renewal and healing; the need for revival; the need for a new love of the Word of God.

Nor were my talks exclusively about the Kingdom of God in Troyan. I shared about the Gospel in Vietnam and Pakistan. I talked of the dangers of the Islamic Revolution—*before* 9/11. I warned of the subtle seduction of

Western Materialism, at a time when half the population of Bulgaria would have loved to have come and lived in England. I tried to explain how the poor in Troyan had treasure we couldn't buy in the West.

What turned out to be my final talk was actually a summary of some of the Biblical insights concerning Healing that God had taught me in Troyan.

One: They all came to Jesus.

Jesus never went looking for 'business'; the 'business' came looking for Him. They came alone and they came in crowds. They came during the day and in the dead of night. They shouted from a distance and they fell at His feet.

Only when the sick person couldn't travel did another go in his stead; and they were either fathers or masters. No one came to Jesus with lists of people to pray for. The responsibility was always placed on the sick person to " seek the Lord while He may be found." Has the modern phenomena of "would you like us to pray for you at our next meeting" any Biblical basis?

The sick personally seek out the doctor, and submit to his examination. That is the New Testament pattern for healing. We should encourage the sick to go to the meeting themselves and kneel at Jesus' feet. And when the sick are too ill to do that, James provides the answer:

"Is any one of you sick? He should call the elders of the Church to pray over him and anoint him with oil in the name of the Lord. And the prayer offered in faith will make the sick person well; the Lord will raise him up." (James 5:14,15).

It is often forgotten that James is writing to Christians. But why not for everybody? Because although the Lord does heal unbelievers, He has a higher priority for their lives, namely, Salvation through the Blood of His Son. Jesus said to His Disciples; "What good will it be for a man if he gains the whole world, yet forfeits his soul?" (Matthew 16:26).

Two: They were Desperate.

Everyone who came to Jesus for healing was desperate. The Lepers were so desperate they came out of the boundaries of their colonies and risked stoning. (The townsfolk had a legal right to throw stones at them, to protect themselves from the disease.) In desperation they risked making Jesus unclean by touching him (Mark 1:41). Some were so desperate they had spent their life-savings looking for a cure. The Gentiles and tax-gatherers and soldiers were prepared to face rejection and ridicule to get to Him.

The friends of the lame man, seeing the doorway to the house meeting blocked by the crowd, stumbled up the outside steps of the house with the stretcher. There, on the flat roof, they smashed open a hole to lower him down. How desperate can you get? Imagine the outrage of the owner, sending up servants to stop the damage. Imagine the struggle that must have ensued on the roof! Imagine the bill they would have had to pay! They were prepared to do almost anything to get him to Jesus. It doesn't get much more desperate than that.

Three: They had faith.

They knelt at Jesus' feet and called him "Lord". The title was given only to the Roman Emperor, Caesar, or a man of extreme high office. We have no English translation of this word, and therefore our understanding now is a religious one. The nearest translation in old English is "sire", a word used by the serfs (slaves) of medieval England when addressing their masters. Later, the Biblical term was used as a title for the Master – the 'Lord' of the Manor.

The title "Lord" has always been used of the relationship between slave and master. To call someone "Lord" is, in effect, to make yourself his slave. It is to submit to his total sovereignty over your life, including his authority over when you should live and when you should die.

Those who fell at Jesus' feet and cried out "Lord" knew He could heal or not heal. "If you are willing", the leper cries out," you can make me clean." (Mark 1:40). Everything is within the sovereign Lordship of Jesus.

Among those who had known Jesus really well for years, faith was lacking. His Nazareth friends and neighbours – as well as His own brothers and sisters! – who had lived alongside this small businessman (Carpenter), were indifferent, if not openly hostile, to His teaching and ministry. They took offence at what He both said and did (Matthew 13:53-58). Faith was lacking.

Amazingly, Jesus taught that we need very little "faith", providing it comes from the heart and not the head. Unfortunately, there are those in the 'healing business' today who teach the opposite: 'if you have enough faith then God will heal you!' Jesus **never** taught like this. Instead of discouraging us with doubts about our own faith ('you don't have enough'), Jesus taught that a tiny amount was all you needed. He used his Middle Eastern sense of humour to illustrate the point:

"I tell you the truth, if you have faith as small as a mustard seed (i.e. tiny), you can say to this mountain, 'Move from here to there' and it will move. Nothing will be impossible for you." (Matthew 17 :20).

When praying for the sick Jesus never – not once! – told anyone they needed more faith. Instead He encouraged them, and those around who were watching and listening: "Take heart, daughter, your faith has healed you."(Matthew 9:22); "'According to your faith will it be done to you;' and their sight was restored." (Matthew 9:29); "woman, you have great faith. Your request is granted."(Matthew 15:28).

Four: They were repentant

What do we mean by "repentant"? How easy is it for us to get locked inside our own religious jargon. It means that those who came to Jesus came unconditionally. They were not holding anything back ......even their own lives. They were willing to be not only physically healed, but have their lives transformed. And for many, that healing would be a life-changing transformation.

The Lepers would have had their lives turned upside down. Not only had they their best friends, and sometimes family, in the colonies; but also businesses and homes, and even social status in that community. It would all have had to be left behind. And that would have been but the start of their problems. Who in the 'clean' world would want to employ an ex-leper, even after the all clear from the priest? Even if they had family to return to, would the family receive back someone with fingers and nose and toes wasted away? And what about the neighbours? It took real courage to be willing to turn their backs on the security of life in the Colony. Repentance is trusting that Jesus has a plan for you, and trusting Him totally with it. *It is the removing from one's life of everything that is not in that plan.*

Look also at the cost of healing for the crippled beggar (Acts. 3). Begging was the only thing he ever knew. He had steadily built up this 'business', and now was in the top job! The pitch at the Beautiful Gate entrance to the Temple was one of the richest begging pitches in the whole of Jerusalem. All the wealthy Jewish tourists would walk past his feet. Presumably he paid protection money to the local Roman soldiers to keep his competitors away! Who would want to give up a career like that?

This beggar would have seen Jesus and the Disciples many times walking in and out of the Temple precincts. He would have heard all the rumours about the Holy Spirit coming at Pentecost, and seen the transformed faces of many of the 3,000 who converted at that one day. In his heart he wanted something more than to be the richest beggar in Jerusalem. And on this particular day, when Peter and John came by, the Holy Spirit came by also! As Peter told him to get up in the name of Jesus, and took hold of his arm, it was the beggar who put his foot forward and put his weight on it. It was the beggar who had repented of his life, given it all to Jesus, and accepted the gift of healing.

This was not just a physical incident; this was conversion! Here was a man who knew he would have to go back to the family and do a lot of explaining! How were they going to live now? Here was a man who had just trusted the Lord Jesus with his life, with his future, with his family.

Repentance is always the bringing of sin to the Cross and the receiving of forgiveness. But in the New Testament it is more that confession of sins, it is the surrender of one's life.

Five: Jesus healed problems not symptoms.

All family doctors can recount stories of the patient who comes to see them about something trivial, and then just as they are leaving begins: "oh, by the way doctor..." Instinctively, the doctor senses this is the real reason they have come. Unfortunately there are many who come to Jesus for healing who never allow the real problem to be exposed. Jesus didn't need to ask questions, He was the Son of God "who searches hearts and minds" (Rev: 2:23).

So when a mute man was brought to Him, Jesus looked beyond the symptom to the problem. To all around the problem seemed obvious – the man couldn't talk. But Jesus saw something they could not possibly have suspected, that a demonic spirit was controlling the man's ability to speak. "And when the demon was driven out, the man who had been mute spoke" (Matthew 9:33).

Similarly, when the paralytic was lowered before Jesus from the hole in the roof, Jesus could see the problem that no one had noticed – the man's guilt problem. "Son, your sins are forgiven" were the first words he spoke to the young man – and the most important! The sceptical theologians who were listening in on this were immediately offended. The crowd was confused. Could not Jesus see that the man was paralysed? To answer the sceptics, Jesus said a strange thing:

" 'Why are you thinking these things? Which is easier: to say to the paralytic, "your sins are forgiven," or to say, "Get up, take your mat and walk"? But that you may know that the Son of Man has authority on earth to forgive sins...' He said to the paralytic, 'I tell you, get up, take your mat and go home.' He got up, took his mat and walked out in full view of them all. This amazed everyone and they praised God saying, 'We have never seen anything like this!' " (Mark 2:8-12)

It was through the forgiving of this man's sins that the guilt problem was removed. The guilt was at the root of his paralysis. His inability to walk was the symptom of a deeper problem. That is why Jesus said in effect 'I will prove I can forgive sins (the problem) by healing his paralysis (the symptom). Remove the problem and the symptom is so easy to heal. No wonder the crowd gasped: "we have never seen anything like this."

When we pray we need to be led by the Spirit of God. It is Jesus exercising His ministry in and through us by His almighty power. But we still need to ask questions. We need the information that the Son of God when He was on this earth already had. He knew everything about us. For us it is the Holy Spirit who helps us in our questioning to bring the truth into the light. We need to ask questions.

The biggest frustration for a believer who is desperate, who has 'come to Jesus', who has faith and is repentant, is the minister who prays for the symptom! What is more disheartening than going away empty? It is time to learn the lesson.

My time at Troyan had come to an end. I said my goodbyes and departed. These poor brothers and sisters had taken me through so much blessing. I had seen with my own eyes miracles of healing and salvation from the Lord. Amazingly, the writing of this little book is beginning what I believe to be another 'season' of visits to Bulgaria. What is to happen I do not know. But those dear Christians from by first 'season' will forever remain in my heart God's "Miracles in Bulgaria."

ISBN 142512961-7